2019

Michelle

Caitlin J.

Joe & Lora

1000
QUILT INSPIRATIONS

1000

QUILT INSPIRATIONS

Colorful and Creative Designs
for Traditional, Modern,
and Art Quilts

SANDRA SIDER

Quarry Books
100 Cummings Center, Suite 406L
Beverly, MA 01915

quarrybooks.com • craftside.typepad.com

© 2015 by Quarry Books

First published in the United States of America in 2015 by
Quarry Books, a member of
Quarto Publishing Group USA Inc.
100 Cummings Center
Suite 406-L
Beverly, Massachusetts 01915-6101
Telephone: (978) 282-9590
Fax: (978) 283-2742
www.quarrybooks.com
Visit www.Craftside.Typepad.com for a behind-the-scenes peek at our crafty world!

10 9 8 7 6 5 4 3 2 1

ISBN: 978-1-59253-984-0

Digital edition published in 2015
eISBN: 978-1-62788-310-8

Library of Congress Control Number: 2014946917

Design: Claire MacMaster | barefoot art graphic design
Cover Image: (front, clockwise from top left): Denise Oyama Miller, Barbara Littlefield Wendt, Sheila Frampton-Cooper, Victoria Adams Brown, Teresa Shippy, Katie Pasquini Masopust, Robbie Payne; Terry Aske; (spine) Candice Phelan; (back) Patricia R Charity

Printed in China

In memory of Virginia Dare Saunders,
my paternal grandmother, an Appalachian quilt maker extraordinaire.

Contents

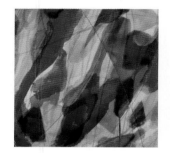

Introduction

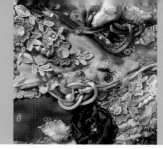

Many quilters find their inspiration in other quilts, from an appealing family heirloom to an art quilt in a gallery show. Although this book has four distinct sections—traditional, modern, pictorial, and abstract and conceptual art quilts—I encourage you to browse all the images regardless of your quilting style. An art quilt might feature jazzy color combinations that could transform a traditional pattern, and a traditional-style work might suggest texture and tonal values to a quilt artist. Modern quilters, such as members of the Modern Quilt Guild, design mainly with solid colors and often adapt traditional patterns in innovative ways, finding their inspiration in every aspect of today's quilts. While most of the images in this book show quilt details, several are of miniature quilts.

From Colonial mosaic quilts to dynamically graphic Amish quilts to the asymmetrical explosions of African-American makers, pieced quilts have played an important role in the development of quilt making in the U.S. By the mid-nineteenth century, quilts pieced in modular blocks were becoming popular, especially star patterns, fan motifs, and log cabin designs. Many contemporary makers rely on modular structure, occasionally using tessellation and fractals. While pieced quilts, especially those featuring curved quilting, comprise a variety of designs, the majority favor a grid format. This type of structure presents an opportunity for secondary patterns to be created where the corners and edges of blocks meet.

From historic Baltimore album quilts to whole-cloth Hawaiian beauties to the extravagant patriotic examples celebrating the U.S. Bicentennial, ornamental appliquéd quilts have long been considered show quilts. Although intricately stitched floral appliqués waned in popularity by the mid-nineteenth century, commemorative appliquéd quilts flourished into the twentieth century, celebrating individuals such as military heroes and suffragettes and depicting historic places and events in narrative style. Lithographic images and text printed on cloth, usually silk, enhanced these appliquéd compositions. Traditionally, appliquéd quilts have required many thousands of tiny stitches by hand. Today, with processes such as fusing to position motifs, design software, and equipment such as computer-driven sewing machines, numerous quilt makers use appliqué to produce organic designs. Traditional makers often use appliquéd blocks to create sampler quilts, or assemble identical blocks around a central medallion.

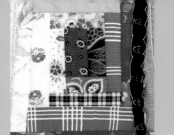

The most famous examples of mixed techniques in historic quilt making can be found in nineteenth-century crazy quilts, often combining piecing, appliqué, and embellishment in the form of ornate hand embroidery, buttons, badges, ribbons, portraits, floral sculpture in fabric, and even small stuffed animals. Many crazy quilts have a modular structure, assembled in blocks, but sometimes the structure disappears beneath a web of embellishment.

Today's quilt artists, such as members of Studio Art Quilt Associates, cast their nets deep and wide in quilt history as well as in modern art for inspiration. Rather than focusing on specific techniques, many of these makers explore process in their work—dyeing, painting, printing, photography, discharge, resist, and so on. Their creativity thrives on the unpredictable patterns and imagery resulting in the fabric. Others rely on commercial textiles, piecing, and appliquéing compositions in a painterly fashion, in abstract or representational modes. A small percentage of quilt artists work conceptually and with unusual materials, such as twist ties, plastic bags, currency, wood, film, and even matchsticks.

Quilting as a structural technique has been employed in textiles worldwide since ancient times. Modular quilt tops, whether in blocks or strips, became an international phenomenon during the twentieth century, with hundreds of quilting groups around the globe proliferating via the Internet in the past two decades. The International Quilt Association has approximately 6,200 members from 38 countries. Today's makers build upon the historical continuum of quilting as individual techniques and styles contribute to the medium. From Japanese *sashiko* to Central American *molas*, the diversity of regional textiles enriches every area of quilting, expanding our appreciation of the craft.

Images in this book come from more than 300 quilt makers from 20 countries, showcasing every imaginable technique and process in today's quilting. We are also privileged to include a selection of details from traditional quilts in the Collection of International Quilt Festival, many of them previously unpublished. Chapter one also presents traditional quilts in the private collection of Werner and Karen Gundersheimer, most previously unpublished. Let your imagination free to roam through these ideas, opening your creativity to new dimensions.

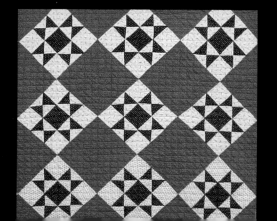

CHAPTER 1

Traditional Designs

0001   Tierney Davis Hogan, USA

0002   Tierney Davis Hogan, USA

0003   Tierney Davis Hogan, USA

0004   Tierney Davis Hogan, USA

0005 Mary Tabar, USA

0006 Mary Tabar, USA

0007 Mary Tabar, USA

0008 Mary Tabar, USA

0009 Frances M. Snay, USA

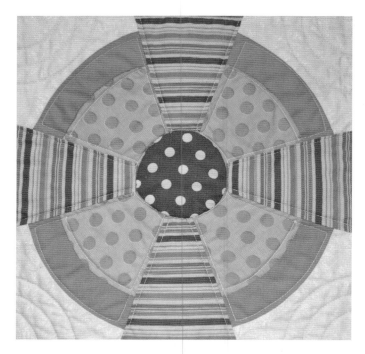

0010 Melanie Grant, USA

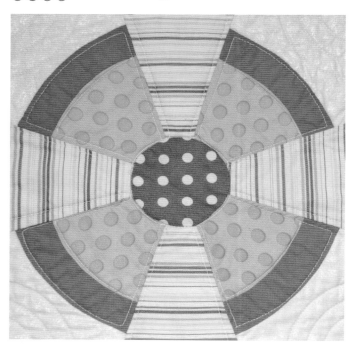

0011 Melanie Grant, USA

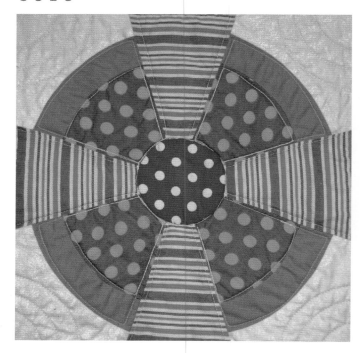

0012 Melanie Grant, USA

0013   W. Jean Ayres, USA

0014   Melanie Grant, USA

0015   Jenny K. Lyon, USA

0016   Barbara Littlefield Wendt, USA

0017   W. Jean Ayres, USA

0018   W. Jean Ayres, USA

0019   Melanie Grant, USA

0020   Melanie Grant, USA

0021   Deanna Miller, USA

0022   Nienke Smit, Netherlands

0023   Melanie Grant, USA

0024   W. Jean Ayres, USA

0025   LeRita McKeever, USA

0026   Darleen N. Madsen, USA

0027   Sarah Cullins, USA

0028   Sarah Cullins, USA

0029   Marjolijn van Wijk, Netherlands

0030   Marjolijn van Wijk, Netherlands

0031   Frances M. Snay, USA

0032   Vicki Bohnhoff, USA

0033 Klaske Witteveen, Netherlands

0034 Klaske Witteveen, Netherlands

0035 Wil Duyst, Netherlands

0036 Wil Duyst, Netherlands

0037 Annemiek Te Pas-Aalders, Netherlands

0038 Annemiek Te Pas-Aalders, Netherlands

0039 Wil Duyst, Netherlands

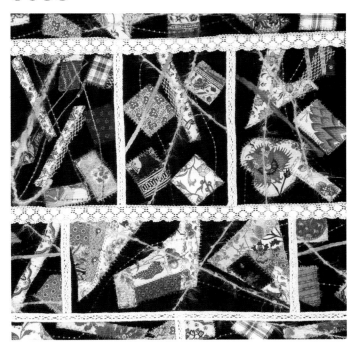

0040 Wil Duyst, Netherlands

0041 Helen Remick, USA

0042 Helen Remick, USA

0043 Helen Remick, USA

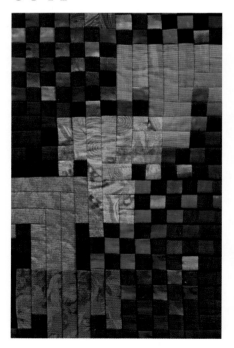

0044 Emiko Toda Loeb, USA

0045 Emiko Toda Loeb, USA

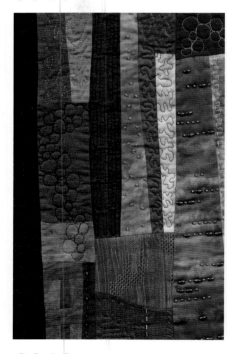

0046 Emiko Toda Loeb, USA

0047   Mary Markworth, USA

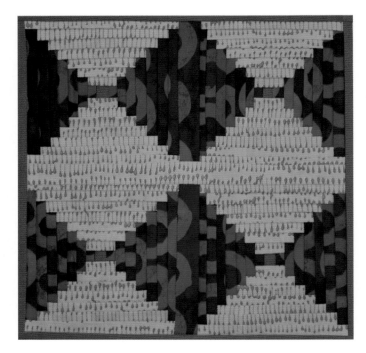

0048   Melanie Grant, USA

0049   Melanie Grant, USA

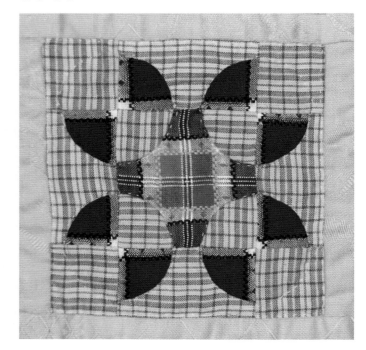

0050   José Beenders, Netherlands

0051   José Beenders, Netherlands

0052 Kristin La Flamme, USA

0053 Catherine Baltgalvis, USA

0054 Jodi Scaltreto, USA

0055 Linda Kittmer, Canada

0056 Brigitte Morgenroth, Germany

0057   LeRita McKeever, USA

0058   Sarah Cullins, USA

0059   Sarah Cullins, USA

0060   Sarah Cullins, USA

0061   Pam Gantz, USA

0062   Nienke Smit, Netherlands

0063   Kathleen Carrizal-Frye, USA

0064   Kathleen Carrizal-Frye, USA

0065 Kathleen Carrizal-Frye, USA

0066 Kathleen Carrizal-Frye, USA

0067 Kathleen Carrizal-Frye, USA

0068 Kathleen Carrizal-Frye, USA

0069 Kathleen Carrizal-Frye, USA

0070   Marjolijn van Wijk, Netherlands

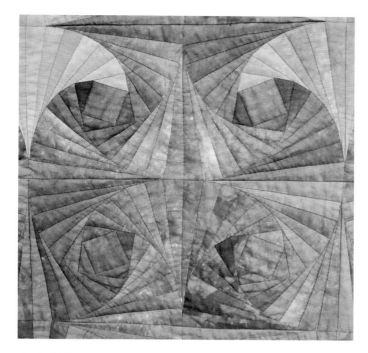

0071 Brigitte Morgenroth, Germany

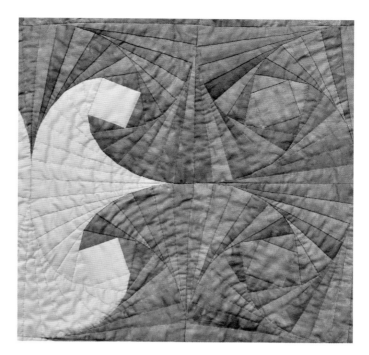

0072 Brigitte Morgenroth, Germany

0073 Brigitte Morgenroth, Germany

0074 Brigitte Morgenroth, Germany

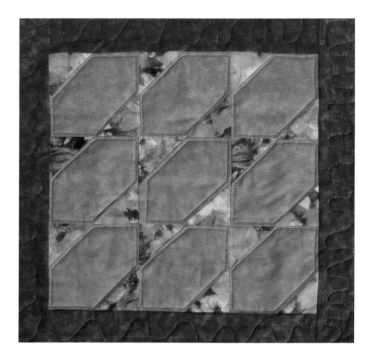

0075 Cindy Richard, Israel

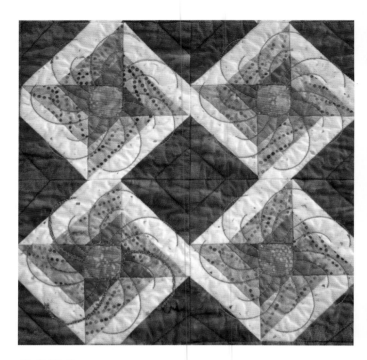

0076 Mary Markworth, USA

0077 LeRita McKeever, USA

0078 LeRita McKeever, USA

0079 Diane Becka, USA

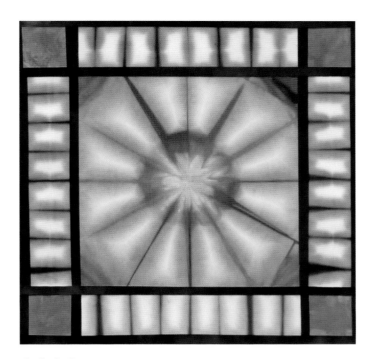

0080 Nienke Smit, Netherlands

0081 Nienke Smit, Netherlands

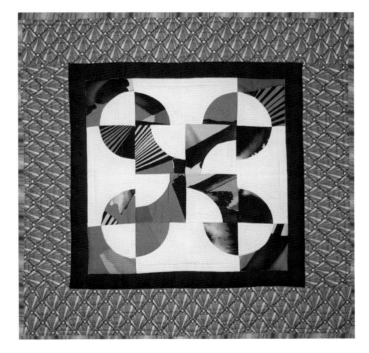

0082 Marven Donati, Canada

0083 Sandy Campbell, USA

0084 Victoria Adams Brown, USA

0085 Victoria Adams Brown, USA

0086 Victoria Adams Brown, USA

0087 Victoria Adams Brown, USA

0088   Robbie Payne, USA

0089   W. Jean Ayres, USA

0090   W. Jean Ayres, USA

0091   W. Jean Ayres, USA

0092   W. Jean Ayres, USA

0093   W. Jean Ayres, USA

0094   Shelly Burge, USA

0095   W. Jean Ayres, USA

0096   W. Jean Ayres, USA

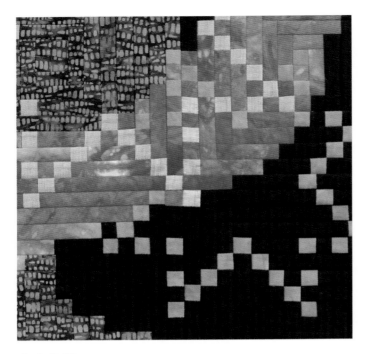

0097 Emiko Toda Loeb, USA

0098 Emiko Toda Loeb, USA

0099 Emiko Toda Loeb, USA

0100 Emiko Toda Loeb, USA

0101   Emiko Toda Loeb, USA

0102　Noriko Misawa, Japan

0103   Noriko Misawa, Japan

0104   Watanabe Kayoko, Japan

0105   Watanabe Kayoko, Japan

0106   Watanabe Kayoko, Japan

0107   Jolene Mershon, USA

0108   Jolene Mershon, USA

0109   Jolene Mershon, USA

0110   Jolene Mershon, USA

0111 Shelly Burge, USA

0112 Shelly Burge, USA

0113 Wil Duyst, Netherlands

0114 Geraldine A. Wilkins, USA

0115 Laura Bisagna, USA

0116 Akiko Hayata/New Zephyrs, Japan

0117 Nienke Smit, Netherlands

0118 Geraldine A. Wilkins, USA

0119 Masae Harata, Japan

0120 Masae Harata, Japan

0121 Pamela Mansfield, USA

0122 Gail P. Sims, USA

0123 Jolene Mershon, USA

0124 Jolene Mershon, USA

0125 Helene Kusnitz, USA

0126 Luisa Marina, Spain

0127 Elayne Novotny, USA

0128 Wil Duyst, Netherlands

0129 Brigitte Morgenroth, Germany

0130 Barbara Triscari, USA

0131 Vicki Conley, USA

0132   Luisa Marina, Spain

0133   Jenny K. Lyon, USA

0134   Judy Doolan Kjellin, Sweden

0135   Jen Sorenson, USA

1000 QUILT INSPIRATIONS

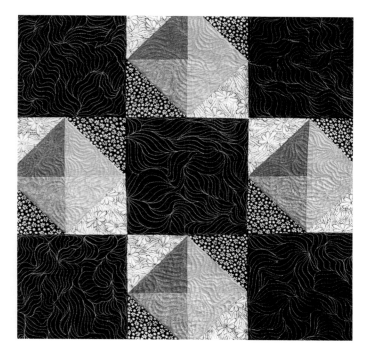

0136   Geraldine A. Wilkins, USA

0137   Diane Becka, USA

0138   Diane Becka, USA

0139   Diane Becka, USA

0140   Carol Anne Grotrian, USA

0141   Sarah Ann Smith, USA

0142   Catherine Baltgalvis, USA

Collection of International Quilt Festival

These images come from traditional quilts, many being exceptional nineteenth-century examples, from the Collection of International Quilt Festival. Vicki Mangum, registrar for the Texas Quilt Museum, co-curated this section of the book. We are very grateful to Karey Patterson Bresenhan and Nancy O'Bryant Puentes, founders of the collection, for permission to publish these details from their quilts. Most of the photographs are by Jim Lincoln.

0143 Feathered Stars & Redwork, c. 1900

0144 Star Spangled Banner, c. 1860

0145 Scherenschnitte Quilt, c. 1895

0146 Birds & Grapes Appliqué, c. 1870

0147 Pine Tree, c. 1880

0148 Rose of Sharon, variation, c. 1860

0149   Pots of Flowers with Stars, c. 1860

0150   North Carolina Lily with Sunflowers

0151   Single Irish Chain

0152   Ohio Star with Sawtooth Border, c. 1880

0153 Pineapple Appliqué, c. 1890; 2003

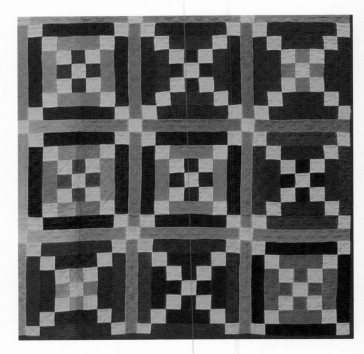

0154 Nine Patch Criss-Cross, c. 1895

0155 Touching Stars, c. 1865

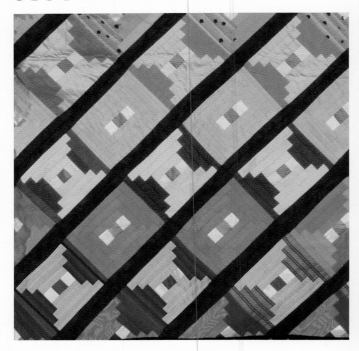

0156 Silk Victorian Log Cabin, c. 1890

0157   Pineapple Log Cabin, c. 1890

0158   New York Beauty, c. 1930

0159   Nine Patch Variation, 1920

0160   Lover's Knot, c. 1940

0161 Sampler, c. 1880; 2003

0162 Log Cabin with Star Center

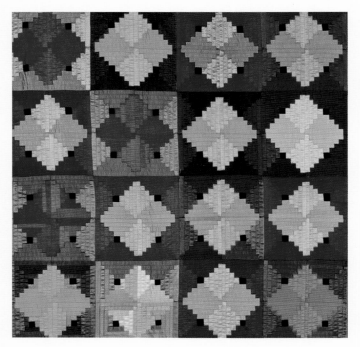

0163 Log Cabin, Courthouse Steps, variation, c. 1890

0164 Spiderweb, c. 1900

0165 Garden Maze with Shoo Fly, c. 1870

0166 Contained Crazy Quilt, c. 1850–1875

0167 Log Cabin with Ohio Stars, c. 1900

0168 President's Medallion, c. 1889

0169 Vase of Tulips, c. 1930

0170 Hawaiian Floral Urns, c. 1930

0171 Prairie Flower, c. 1870

0172 Whig Rose

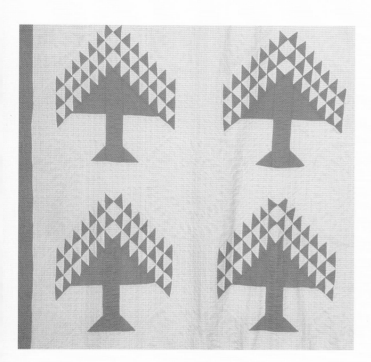

0173   Pine Tree, c. 1930

0174   Hawaiian Appliqué, white on green, c. 1930

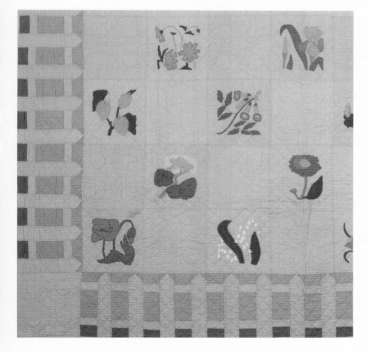

0175   Floral Picket Fence, c. 1930

0176   Flower Garden, c. 1930

The Gundersheimer Collection

Karen and Werner Gundersheimer, (married in 1963), grew up outside Philadelphia, both with a love of the arts. Karen, who illustrated and/or wrote more than thirty children's books, bought her first vintage quilt in 1954 at the age of 15. Werner, whose taste ran more to old master painting, was drawn to folk art during a research stay in Italy in the mid-1960s. Together, Karen and Werner discovered a deep admiration for women's work—embroidery and quilts—that became an enduring passion. Their interest in early quilts grew into a central focus of their collecting energies, which soon expanded to embrace painted furniture as well as works of art by contemporary and early folk and outsider artists in a wide range of media. Yet quilts always remained at or near the heart of the Gundersheimers' enterprise—an attraction irresistible for vivid geometries, appealing color, and wonderful techniques.

0177   Friendship Album

0178   Roman Stripe

0179   Star of Bethlehem, Mennonite quilt (1920s)

0180   Joseph's Coat, Mennonite quilt (early-twentieth century)

0181   Churn Dash (1920s)

0182   Pieced Baskets

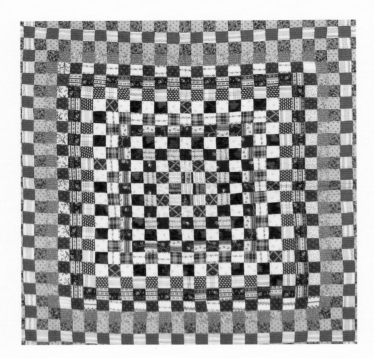

0183 Philadelphia Pavement, Postage Stamp (1930s)

0184 Trip Around the World, Mennonite quilt (1920s)

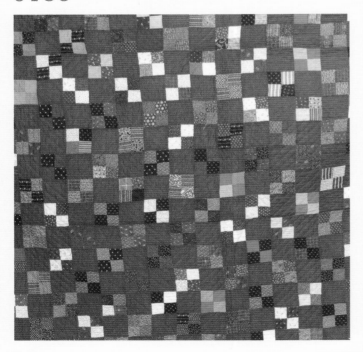

0185 Four Patch (1920s)

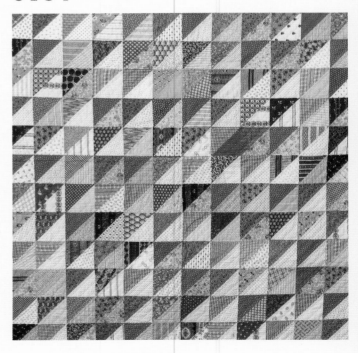

0186 Triangles Quilt (1930s)

0187   Broken Dishes, Variation (1930s)

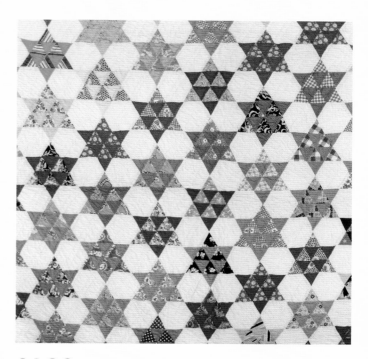

0188   Touching Stars, c. 1935

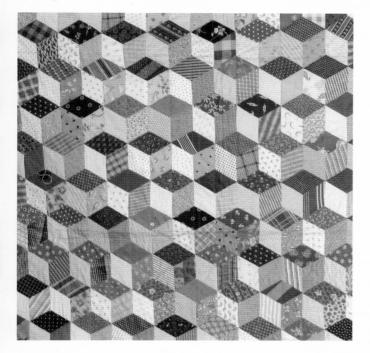

0189   Tumbling Blocks (1920s)

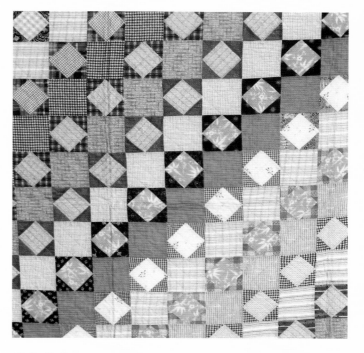

0190   Jacob's Ladder, variation (1930s)

0191 Roman Stripe (1920s)

0192 Lozenge quilt (1930s)

0193 Ocean Waves, Mennonite quilt (1930s)

0194 Pinwheel (1920s)

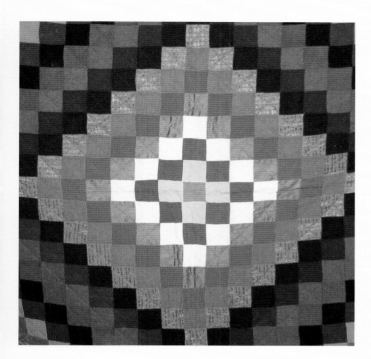

0195   Sunshine and Shadow, Amish quilt (1920s)

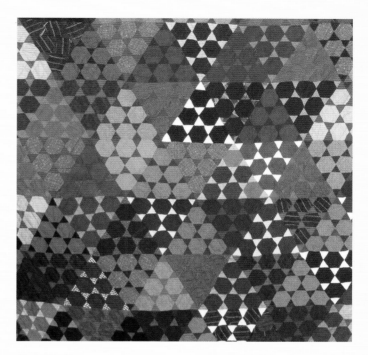

0196   Pyramid quilt, c. 1910

0197   Crazy Quilt in squares (1940s)

0198   Crazy Quilt (late-nineteenth century)

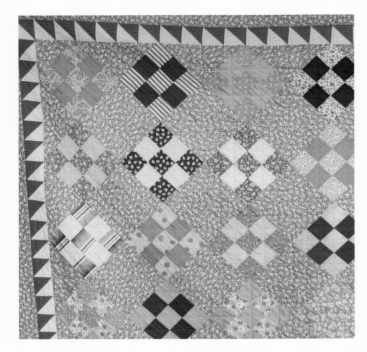

0199   Nine Patch with Sawtooth border, (1930s)

0200   Double Wedding Ring (1930s)

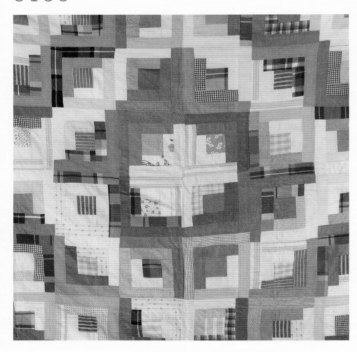

0201   Barn Raising, Log Cabin (1940s)

0202   Drunkard's Path (1920s)

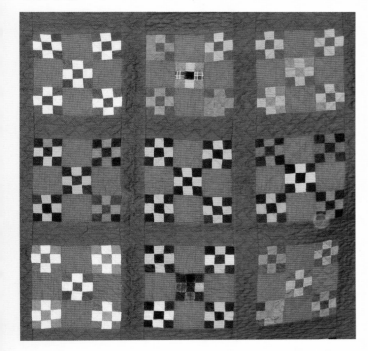

0203   Alphabet quilt (early-twentieth century)

0204   Appliquéd Tulips (1920s)

0205   Double Nine Patch, Amish quilt (1920s)

0206   Broken Star

CHAPTER 2

Modern Designs

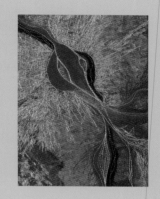

0207   Barbara Littlefield Wendt, USA

0208   Susan Fuller, USA

0209   Susan Fuller, USA

0210   Susan Fuller, USA

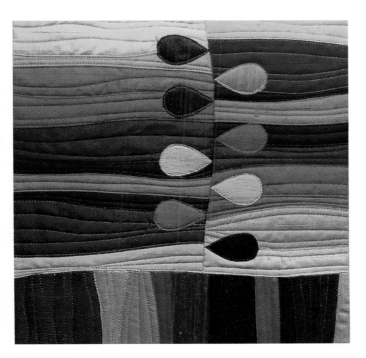

0211 Geri deGruy, USA

0212 Geri deGruy, USA

0213 Geri deGruy, USA

0214 Geri deGruy, USA

0215 Ruth Christos, USA

0216 Ruth Christos, USA

0217 Ruth Christos, USA

0218 Ruth Christos, USA

0219   Ann Grundler, USA

0220   Ann Grundler, USA

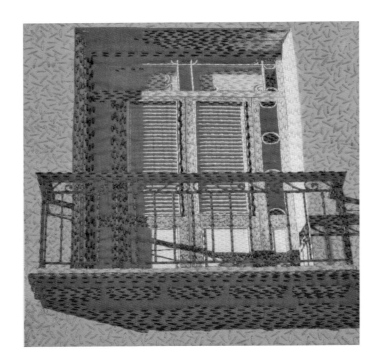

0221   Holly Brackmann, USA

0222   Holly Brackmann, USA

0223   Cindy Grisdela, USA

0224   Denise Oyama Miller, USA

0225   Vivian Helena Aumond-Capone, USA

0226   Shelly Burge, USA

0227   Cheryl Olson, USA

0228   Veronica Oborn Jefferis, Australia

0229   Sheri Schumacher, USA

0230   Sheri Schumacher, USA

0231   Sheri Schumacher, USA

0232   Sheri Schumacher, USA

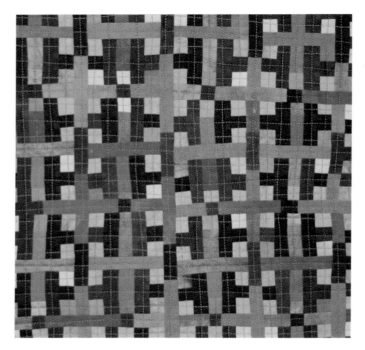

0234   Eleanor A. McCain, USA

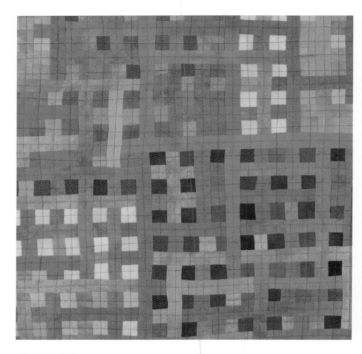

0235   Eleanor A. McCain, USA

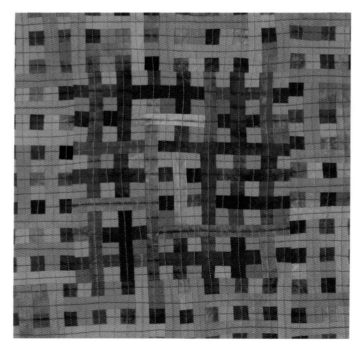

0236   Eleanor A. McCain, USA

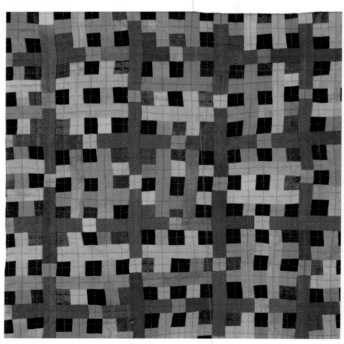

0237   Eleanor A. McCain, USA

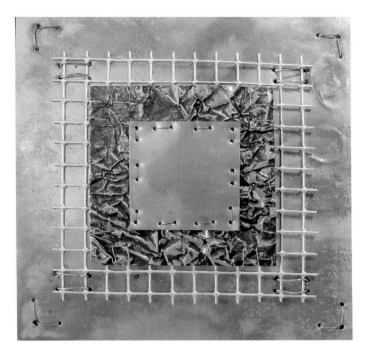

0238   Dianne Gibson, Canada

0239   Dianne Gibson, Canada

0240   Dianne Gibson, Canada

0241   Dianne Gibson, Canada

0242 Joan Dyer, USA

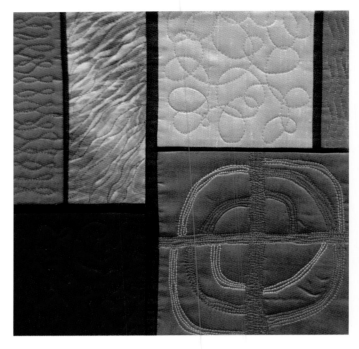

0243 Joan Dyer, USA

0244 Joan Dyer, USA

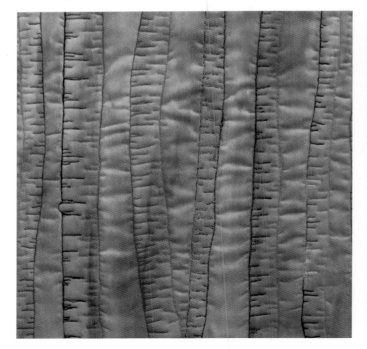

0245 Joan Dyer, USA

0246 Tierney Davis Hogan, USA

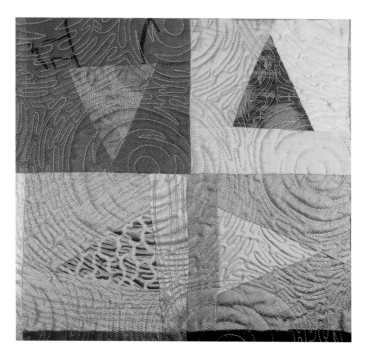

0247 Tierney Davis Hogan, USA

0248 Tierney Davis Hogan, USA

0249 Tierney Davis Hogan, USA

0250   **Hilde Morin, USA**

0251   **Hilde Morin, USA**

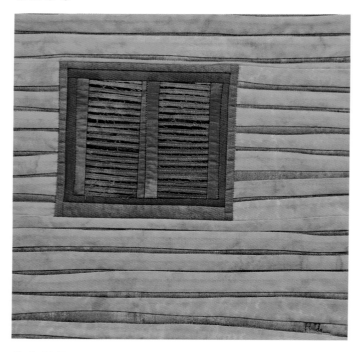

0252   **Hilde Morin, USA**

0253   **Hilde Morin, USA**

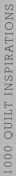

0254   Jean Renli Jurgenson, USA

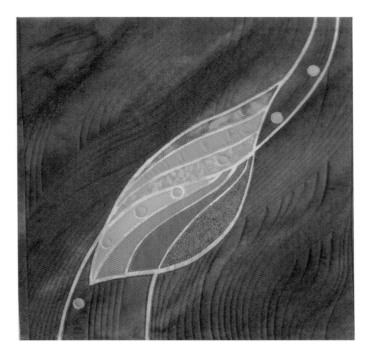

0255   Jean Renli Jurgenson, USA

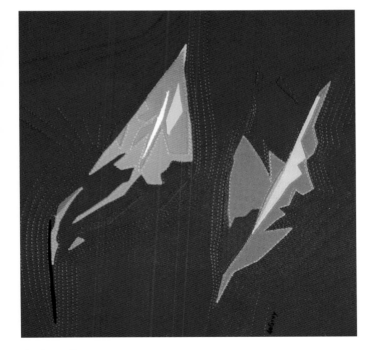

0256   Geri deGruy, USA

0257   Shelly Burge, USA

0258   Frieda Oxenham, UK

0259   Henrietta L. Mac, USA

0260   Henrietta L. Mac, USA

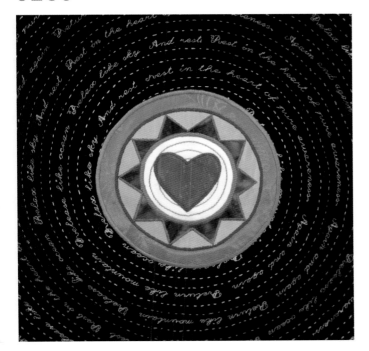

0261   Sharon Willas Rubuliak, Canada

0262   Sharon Willas Rubuliak, Canada

0263 Diane Melms, USA

0264 Diane Melms, USA

0265 Diane Melms, USA

0266 Diane Melms, USA

0267 Karin Wallgren, USA

0268 Karin Wallgren, USA

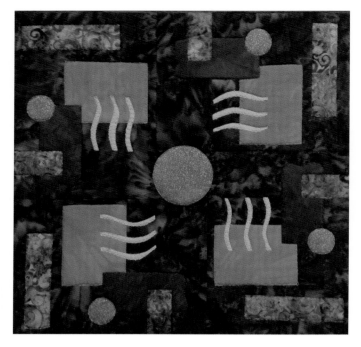

0269   Becky Grover, USA

0270   Christine Seager, UK

0271   Christine Seager, UK

0272   Christine Seager, UK

0273   Phyllis Small, USA

0274   Karen Farmer, UK

0275   Geri deGruy, USA

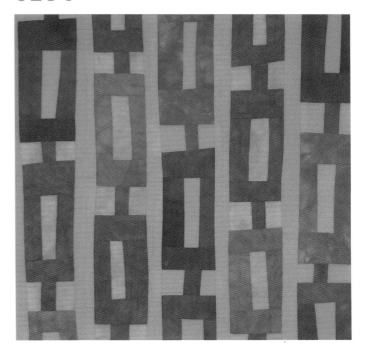

0276   Brenda Gael Smith, Australia

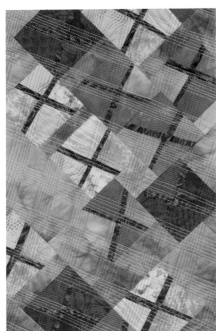

0277 Marti Plager, USA

0278 Marti Plager, USA

0279 Marti Plager, USA

0280 Clara Nartey, USA

0281 Clara Nartey, USA

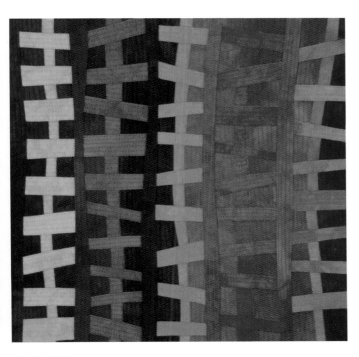

0282 Brenda Gael Smith, Australia

0284 Brenda Gael Smith, Australia

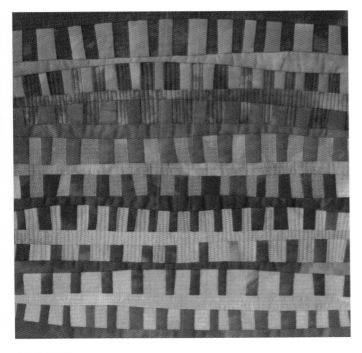

0283 Brenda Gael Smith, Australia

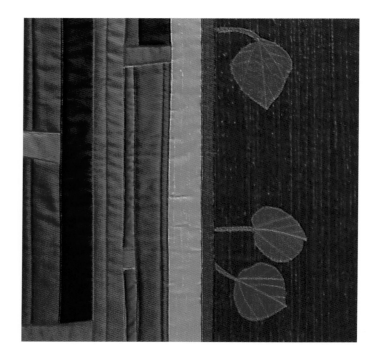

0285 Geri deGruy, USA

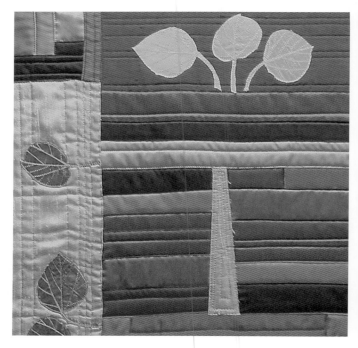

0286 Geri deGruy, USA

0287 Geri deGruy, USA

0288 Geri deGruy, USA

0289 Geri deGruy, USA

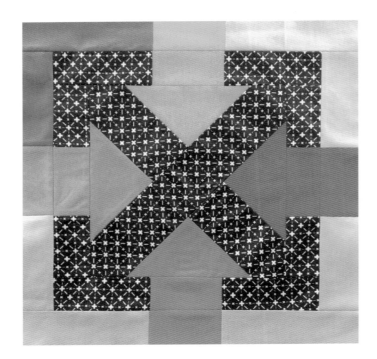

0290 Michelle Wilkie, USA

0291 Michelle Wilkie, USA

0292 Shelly Burge, USA

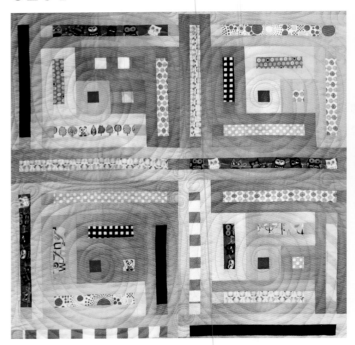

0293 Kimberly Lapacek, USA

0294 Sherri Lipman McCauley, USA

0295 Susan Jackan, USA

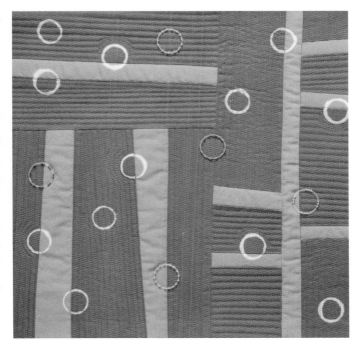

0296 Shelly Burge, USA

0297 Frieda Oxenham, UK

0298 Shelly Burge, USA

0299 Cynthia H. Catlin, USA

0300 Berta Goldbager, USA

0301 Shelly Burge, USA

0302   Linda Bilsborrow, UK

0303   Odette Tolksdorf, South Africa

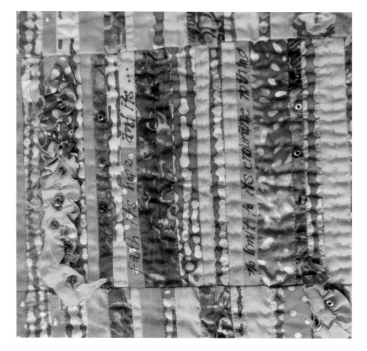

0304   Janie Krig, USA

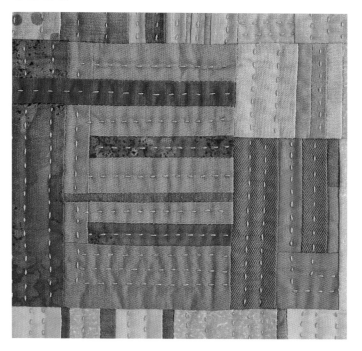

0305   Odette Tolksdorf, South Africa

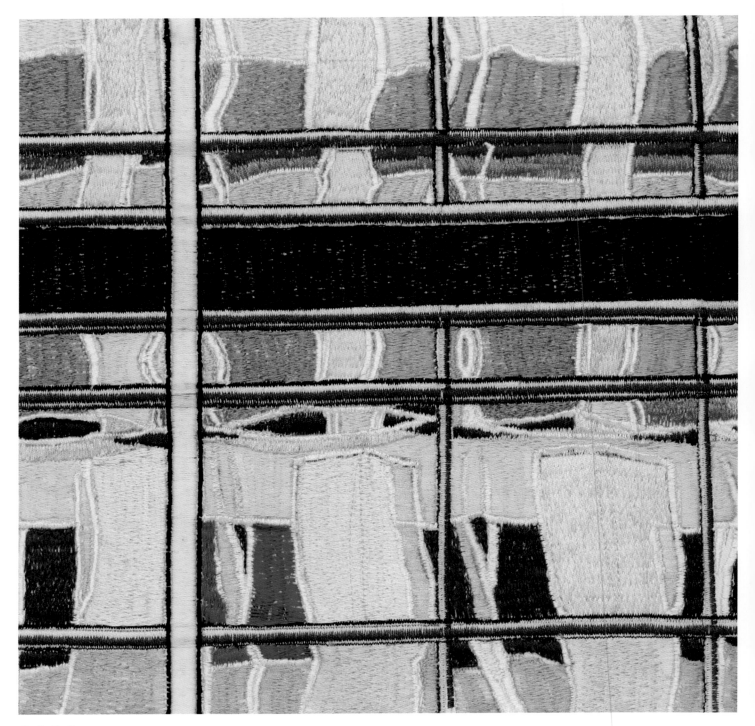

0306 B J Adams, USA

0307   B J Adams, USA

0308   Uta Lenk, Germany

0309   B J Adams, USA

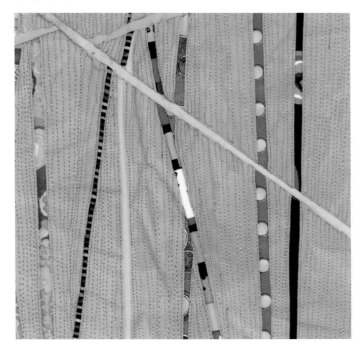

0310   Linda Kittmer, Canada

0311 B J Adams, USA

0312 B J Adams, USA

0313 Karen Farmer, UK

0314 Cindy Richard, Israel

0315 Linda Robertus, Australia

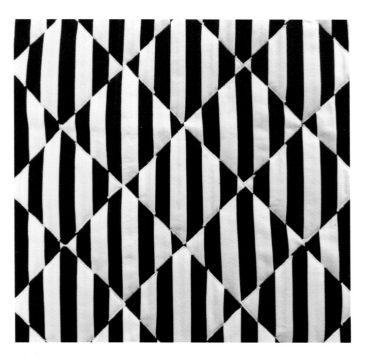

0316 Linda Robertus, Australia

0317 Geri deGruy, USA

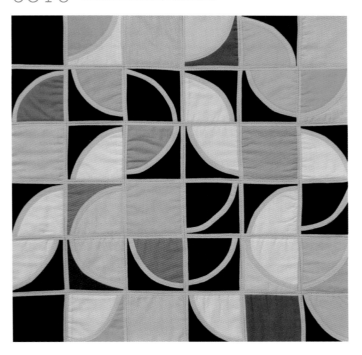

0318 Melanie Grant, USA

0319   Linda Anderson, USA

0320   Elaine Millar, USA

0321   Helen Remick, USA

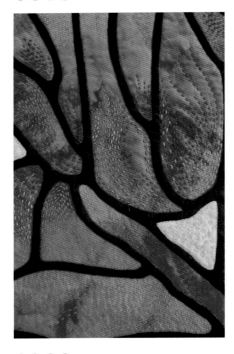

0322   Robbie Payne, USA

0323   Marjorie Post, USA

0324   Marjorie Post, USA

0325   Terry Waldron, USA

0326   Terry Waldron, USA

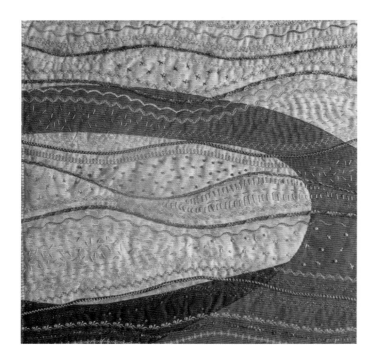

0327   Shirley MacGregor, USA

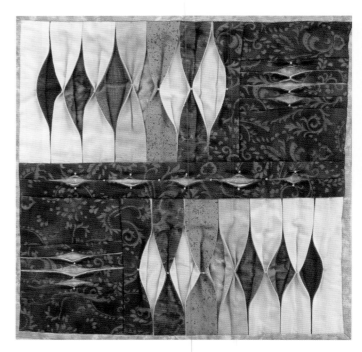

0328   Jill Sheehan, USA

0329   Linda Robertus, Australia

0330   Heidi Zielinski, USA

0331   Wendy Harris Williams, Canada

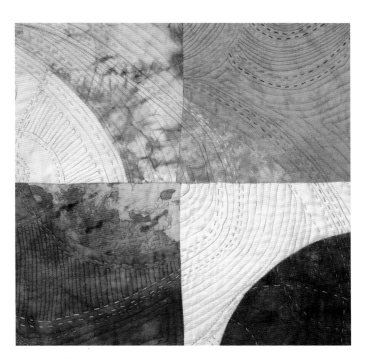

0332   Bobbe Shapiro Nolan, USA

0333   Robin Ryan, USA

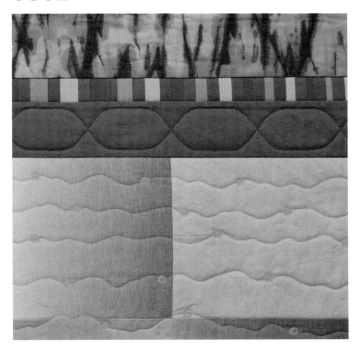

0334   Shelly Burge, USA

0335   Brenda Gael Smith, Australia

0336   Odette Tolksdorf, South Africa

0337   Brenda Gael Smith, Australia

0338   Brenda Gael Smith, Australia

Chartreuse IS a neutral

0339   Kristin La Flamme, USA

0340 Odette Tolksdorf,
South Africa

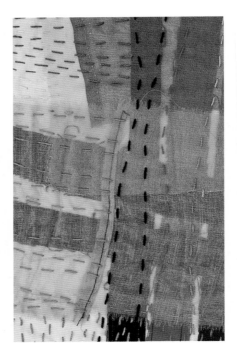

0341 Odette Tolksdorf,
South Africa

0342 Cindy Grisdela, USA

0343 Shelly Burge, USA

0344 Shelly Burge, USA

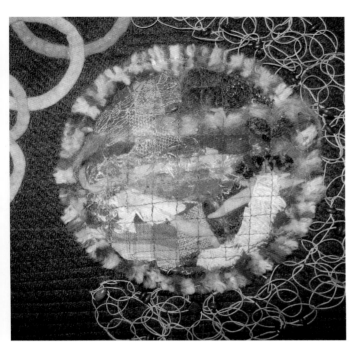

0345   Jana Lalova, Czech Republic

0346   Eleanor A. McCain, USA

0347   Odette Tolksdorf, South Africa

0348   Lisa Walton, Australia

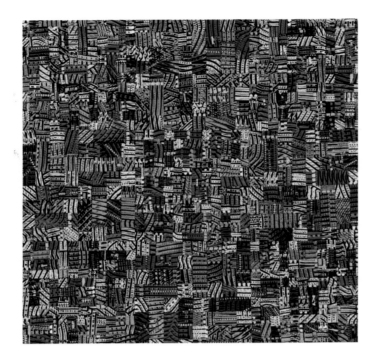

0349   Benedicte Caneill, USA

0350   Cindy Richard, Israel

0351   Dianne Gibson, Canada

0352   Laura Bisagna, USA

0353   Vicki Conley, USA

0354   Jean Brueggenjohann, USA

0355   Geraldine A. Wilkins, USA

0356   Robin DeMuth Schofield, USA

0357   Robin DeMuth Schofield, USA

0358   Geri deGruy, USA

0359   Cheryl Edwards, UK

0360　Geri deGruy, USA

0361　Elena Stokes, USA

0362　Geri deGruy, USA

0363　Geri deGruy, USA

0364   Judith Mundwiler, Switzerland

0365　Vivian Helena Aumond-Capone, USA

0366　Geri deGruy, USA

0367　Elizabeth F. Harris, USA

0368　Christine Ravish, USA

0369 Gerri Spilk, USA

0370 Gerri Spilk, USA

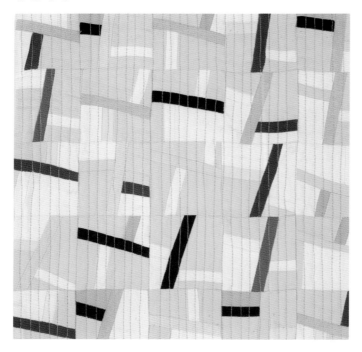

0371 Gerri Spilk, USA

0372 Gerri Spilk, USA

0373　B J Adams, USA

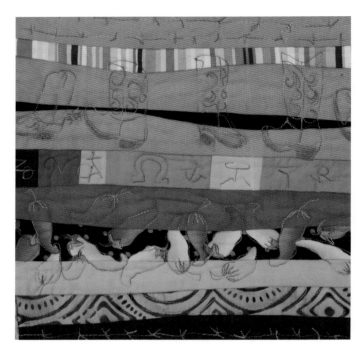

0374 Hope Wilmarth, USA

0375 Hope Wilmarth, USA

0376 Pat Bishop, USA

0377 Pat Bishop, USA

0378　Rhoda Taylor, USA

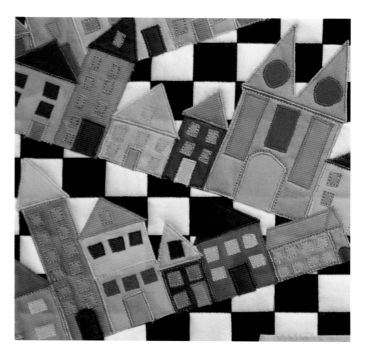

0379　Frieda Oxenham, UK

0380　Rhoda Taylor, USA

0381　Frieda Oxenham, UK

0382 Margie Davidson, Canada

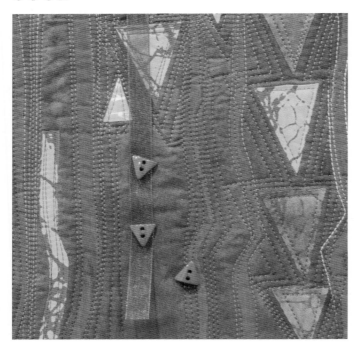

0383 Sherri Lipman McCauley, USA

0384 Candice L. Phelan, USA

0385 Candice L. Phelan, USA

0387 Toni Bergeon, USA

0386 Candice L. Phelan, USA

0388   Patricia Charity, USA

0389   Helene Kusnitz, USA

0390   Gubser Adelheid, Switzerland

0391   Shelly Burge, USA

0392　Katharine McColeman, Canada

0393　Diane Becka, USA

0394　Georgina Newson, UK

0395　Kristin La Flamme, USA

0396   Karen Farmer, UK

0397   Brenda Gael Smith, Australia

0398   Vicki Bohnhoff, USA

0399   Elizabeth Fram, USA

0400   Elizabeth Fram, USA

0401   Elizabeth Fram, USA

0402   Cheryl Olson, USA

0403   Linda Bilsborrow, UK

0404   Holly Brackmann, USA

0405   Odette Tolksdorf,
South Africa

0406   Rhoda Taylor, USA

0407   Dianne Browning, USA

0408   Dianne Browning, USA

0409   Dianne Gibson, Canada

0410 Hope Wilmarth, USA

0411 Sheri Schumacher, USA

0412 Sheri Schumacher, USA

0413 Sheri Schumacher, USA

0414   Mary MacIlvain, USA

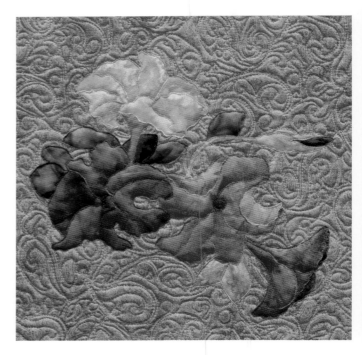

0415   Marjorie Post, USA

0416   Lyric Montgomery Kinard, USA

0417   Melanie Grant, USA

0418 Daniela Tiger, Canada

0419 Marven Donati, Canada

0420 Odette Tolksdorf, South Africa

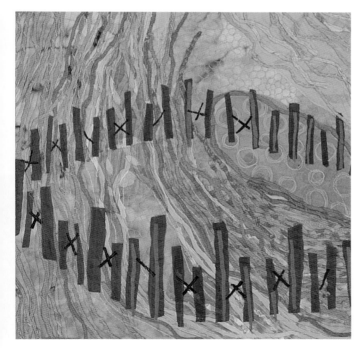

0421 Odette Tolksdorf, South Africa

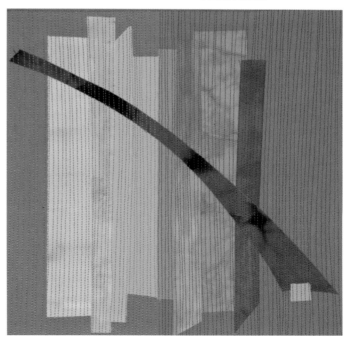

0422 Joanne Alberda, USA

Pictorial Art
Quilt Designs

CHAPTER 3

0423_0679

0423   Denise Oyama Miller, USA

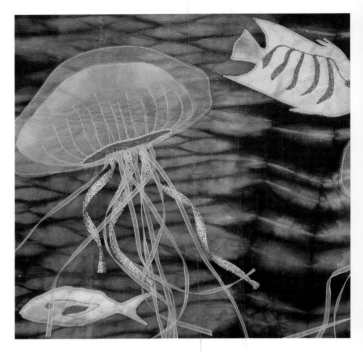

0424   Helene Kusnitz, USA

0425   Pat Owoc, USA

0426   Shannon M. Conley, USA

0427   Tanya A. Brown, USA

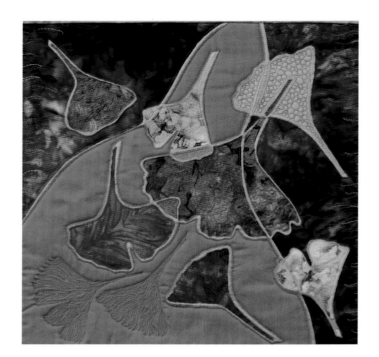

0428 Franki Kohler, USA

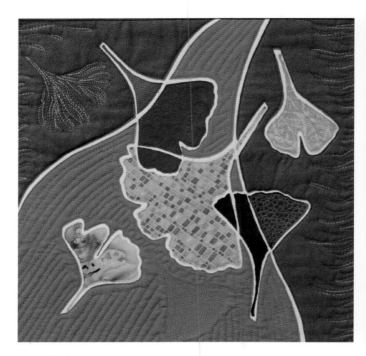

0429 Franki Kohler, USA

0430 Franki Kohler, USA

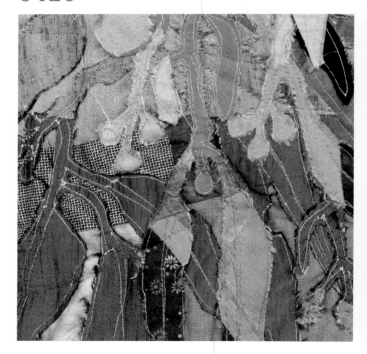

0431 Veronica Oborn Jefferis, Australia

0432   Noriko Endo, Japan

0433   Noriko Endo, Japan

0434   B J Adams, USA

0435   B J Adams, USA

0436 Elisabeth Nacenta-de la Croix, Switzerland

0437 Elisabeth Nacenta-de la Croix, Switzerland

0438 Elisabeth Nacenta-de la Croix, Switzerland

0439 Elisabeth Nacenta-de la Croix, Switzerland

0440　Elisabeth Nacenta-de la Croix, Switzerland

0441   Susan Shie, USA

0442   Susan Shie, USA

0443   Susan Shie, USA

0444   Susan Shie, USA

0445   Terry Aske, Canada

0446   Kim Ritter, USA

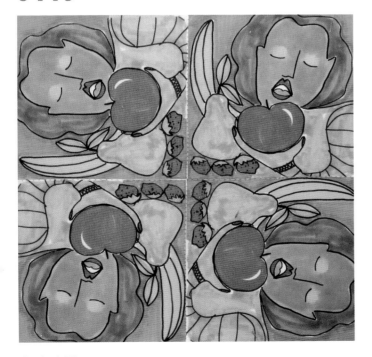

0447   Kim Ritter, USA

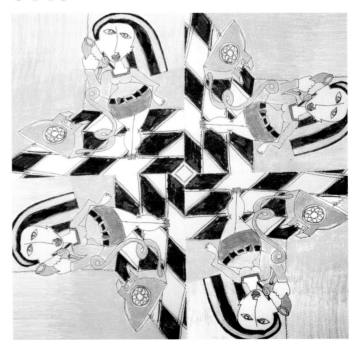

0448   Kim Ritter, USA

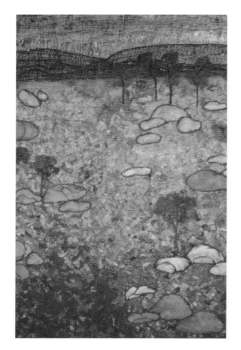

0449   Caroline Sharkey, USA

0450   Caroline Sharkey, Australia

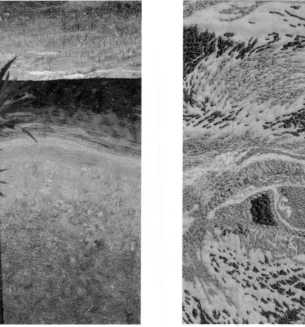

0451   Holly Brackmann, USA

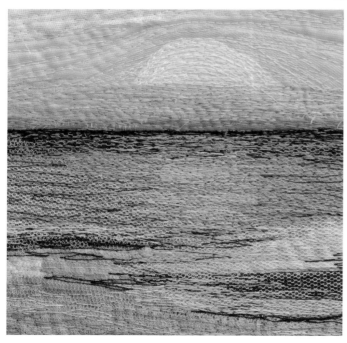

0452   Rebekah Dundon, Australia

0453   Rebekah Dundon, Australia

0454 Jamie Fingal, USA

0455 Denise Oyama Miller, USA

0456 Diane Wright, USA

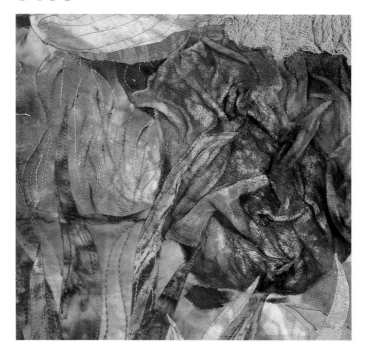

0457 Shelley Brucar, USA

0458 Sylvia Naylor, Canada

0459 Sylvia Naylor, Canada

0460 Sylvia Naylor, Canada

0461 Sylvia Naylor, Canada

0462　Dianne Gibson, Canada

0463　Dianne Gibson, Canada

0464　Arle Sklar-Weinstein, USA

0465　Arle Sklar-Weinstein, USA

144

0466   Ann Baldwin May, USA

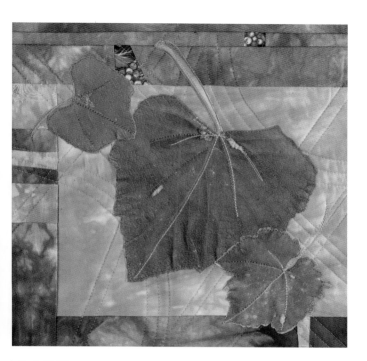

0467   Vivian Helena Aumond-Capone, USA

0468   Gay Young, USA

0469   Sue Reno, USA

0470   Dianne Browning, USA

0471   Elsbeth Nusser-Lampe, Germany

0472   Elsbeth Nusser-Lampe, Germany

0473   Elsbeth Nusser-Lampe, Germany

0474   Dominie Nash, USA

0475   Jenny K. Lyon, USA

0476   Marijke van Welzen, Netherlands

0477   Katie Pasquini Masopust, USA

0478   Holly Altman, USA

0479   Cheryl Olson, USA

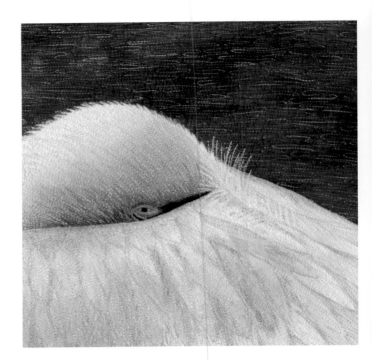

0480   Tanya A. Brown, USA

0481   Kathie Briggs, USA

0482   Carol Seeley, Canada

0483   Melani Kane Brewer, USA

0484   Sara Sharp, USA

0485   Bodil Gardner, Denmark

0486   Julie Duschack, USA

0487   Julie Duschack, USA

0488   Jolene Mershon, USA

0489   Brigitte Kopp, Germany

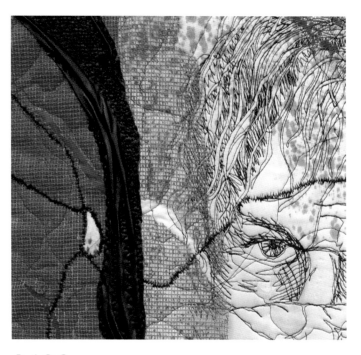

0490   Brigitte Kopp, Germany

0491   Lucy Carroll, Australia

0492   Brigitte Kopp, Germany

0493   Leni Levenson Wiener, USA

0494   Gillian Travis, UK

0495   Linda Robertus, Australia

0496   Leni Levenson Wiener, USA

0497 Leni Levenson Wiener, USA

0498 Leni Levenson Wiener, USA

0499 Linda MacDonald, USA

0500 Linda MacDonald, USA

0501   Patricia Kennedy-Zafred,
USA

0502   Linda Robertus, Australia

0503   Patricia Kennedy-Zafred,
USA

0504   Patricia Kennedy-Zafred, USA

0505   Laurie Swim, Canada

0506 Martha Ressler, USA

0507 Heather DeBreuil, Canada

0508 Heather DeBreuil, Canada

0509 Terry Aske, Canada

0510 Terry Aske, Canada

0511   Terry Aske, Canada

0512   Terry Aske, Canada

0513   Patt Blair, USA

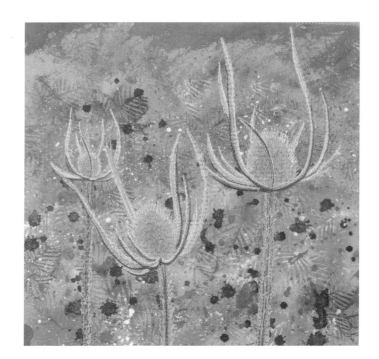

0514   Gillian Travis, UK

0515   Jenny K. Lyon, USA

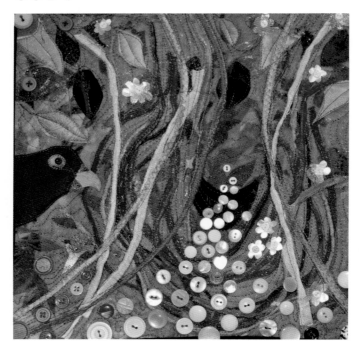

0516   Judith Roderick, USA

0517   Marianne R. Williamson, USA

0518   Nancy Dobson, USA

0519   Nancy Dobson, USA

0520   Rhonda Baldwin, USA

0521   Thelma Newbury, Canada

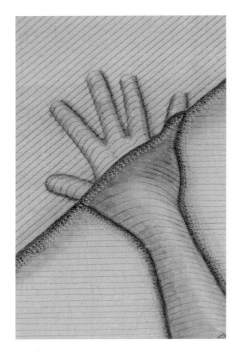

0522 Linda Kittmer, Canada

0523 Arja Speelman, Canada

0524 Deborah Lyn Stanley, USA

0525 Penny Naquin Dant, USA

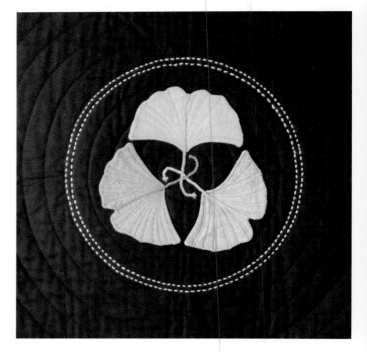

0526 Penny Naquin Dant, USA

0527 Margaret (Meg) Filiatrault, USA

0528 Martha Wolfe, USA

0529 Martha Wolfe, USA

0530 Martha Wolfe, USA

0531 Martha Wolfe, USA

0532   Mary Pal, Canada

0533   Eileen Doughty, USA

0534   Shirley Mooney, New Zealand

0535 Roslyn DeBoer, USA

0536 Roslyn DeBoer, USA

0537 Suze Termaat, Netherlands

0538 Anne Smyers, USA

0539   Eileen Williams, USA

0540   Eileen Williams, USA

0541   Sarah Ann Smith, USA

0542   Marianne R. Williamson, USA

0543 Shelley Brucar, USA

0544 Melani Kane Brewer, USA

0545 Melani Kane Brewer, USA

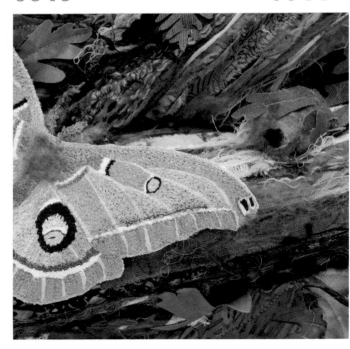

0546 Melani Kane Brewer, USA

0547 Marjolijn van Wijk, Netherlands

0548 Diane Wright, USA

0549 Laurie Swim, Canada

0550 Deb Brockway, USA

0551 Deb Brockway, USA

0552   Mary Tabar, USA

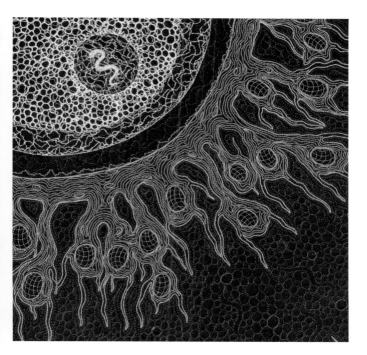

0553 Shea Wilkinson, USA

0554 Shea Wilkinson, USA

0555 Phyllis Small, USA

0556 Carol Marshall, USA

0557 Cheryl Olson, USA

0558 Cheryl Olson, USA

0559 Cheryl Olson, USA

0560 Cheryl Olson, USA

0561 Gwen Goepel, USA

0562 Maxine Oliver, USA

0563 Donna Blum, USA

0564 Vinda G. Robison, USA

0565 Michele Sanandajian, USA

0566 Cindy Richard, Israel

0567 Pat Hertzberg, Canada

0568   Barbara Chapman, Canada

0569   Carolynn McMillan,
Canada

0570   Arja Speelman, Canada

0571   Marijke van Welzen,
Netherlands

0572   Thelma Newbury, Canada

0573   Thelma Newbury, Canada

0574   Nancy Dobson, USA

0575 Susan Selby, Canada

0576 Denise Oyama Miller, USA

0577 Odette Tolksdorf, South Africa

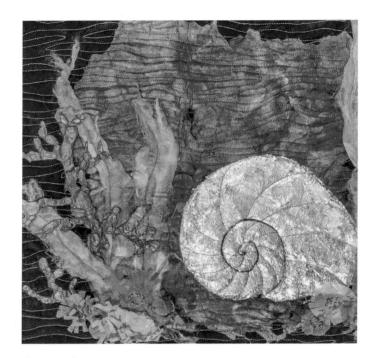

0578 Margaret (Meg) Filiatrault, USA

0579 Anne Smyers, USA

0580 Teresa Shippy, USA

0581 Teresa Shippy, USA

0582   Teresa Shippy, USA

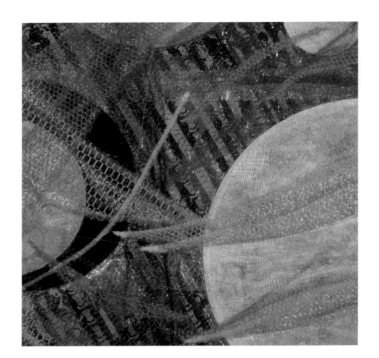

0583   Arturo Alonzo Sandoval, USA

0584   Charlotte Ziebarth, USA

0585   Elizabeth Barton, USA

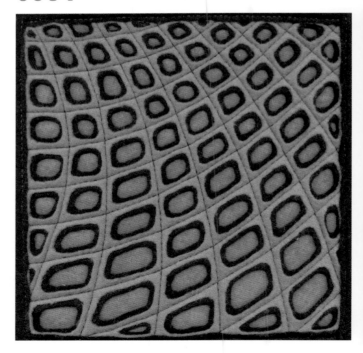

0586   Dianne Firth, Australia

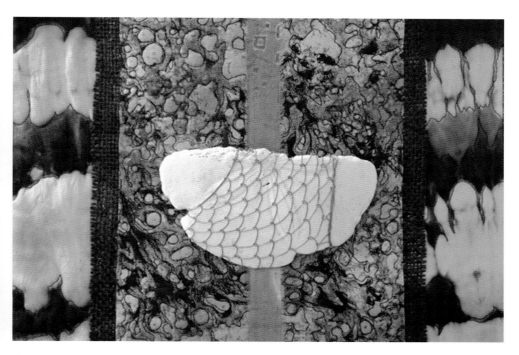

0587   Cathy Spivey Mendola, USA

0588   Linda Stemer, USA

0589   Patricia Gould, USA

0590   Suzanne Mouton Riggio, USA

0591   Arle Sklar-Weinstein, USA

0592   Arturo Alonzo Sandoval, USA

0593   LaVerne Kemp, USA

0594   Jennifer Hammond Landau, USA

0595 Jean Wells Keenan, USA

0596 Kathi Everett, USA

0597 Neroli Henderson, Australia

0598 Nancy Dobson, USA

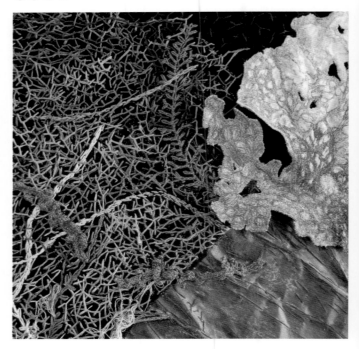

0599 Diane Duncan, Canada

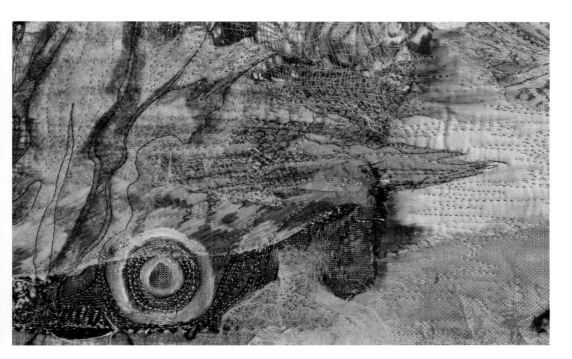

0600   Maya Schonenberger, USA

0601   Maya Schonenberger, USA

0602 Franki Kohler, USA

0603 Franki Kohler, USA

0604 Mary Ann Van Soest, USA

0605 Mary Ann Van Soest, USA

0606   Mary Ann Van Soest, USA

0607   Daniela Tiger, Canada

0608   Candice L. Phelan, USA

0609   Jeanelle McCall, USA

0610   Janneke Van Der Ree, USA

0611   Christine Ravish, USA

0613   Bella Kaplan, Israel

0614   Gillian Travis, UK

0615   Eileen Williams, USA

0616   Sarah Lykins Entsminger, USA

0617   Mary Markworth, USA

0618   Julie Haddrick, Australia

0619   Eileen Williams, USA

0620   Phyllis Small, USA

0621   Els Mommers, Denmark

0622   Arja Speelman, Canada

0623   Nancy Dobson, USA

0624   Ellen Lindner, USA

0625   Katharina Litchman, USA

0626 Carolynn McMillan, Canada

0627 Toni Bergeon, USA

0628 Kristin Shields, USA

0629   Susan Selby, Canada

0630   Sylvia Naylor, Canada

0631   Sylvia Naylor, Canada

0632   Robyn McGrath, Australia

0633   Veronica Oborn Jefferis, Australia

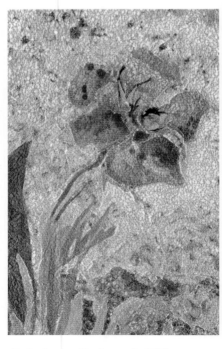

0634   Marianne R. Williamson, USA

0635   Ellen Parrott, USA

0636   Kathie Briggs, USA

0637   Coleen Adderley, Canada

0638   Tanya A. Brown, USA

0639   Victoria Rondeau, USA

0640   Nancy King, USA

0641   Jeanelle McCall, USA

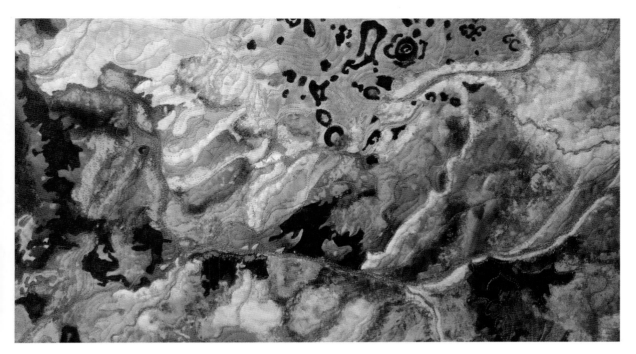

0642 Deb Berkebile, USA

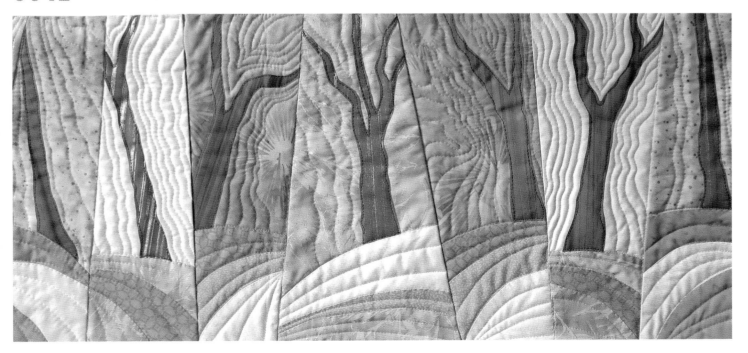

0643 Holly Knott, USA

0644 Dorothy Heidemann-Nelson, USA

0645 Toni Bergeon, USA

0646 Naomi Weidner, USA

0647 Sharon G. Cheney, USA

0648   Pamela Mansfield, USA

0649   Melinda Sword, USA

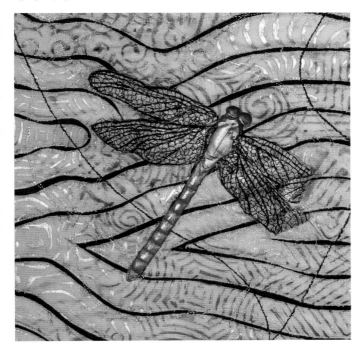

0650   Margaret (Meg) Filiatrault, USA

0651   Jeanelle McCall, USA

0652　Jennifer Bowker, Australia

0653　Jennifer Bowker, Australia

0654　Vita Marie Lovett, USA

0655　Lin Hsin-Chen, Taiwan

0656　Viktorya Allen, USA

0657   Cindy Richard, Israel

0658   Terry Aske, Canada

0659 Donna Blum, USA

0660 Wendy Read, USA

0661 Susan L. Price, USA

0662 Gillian Moss, USA

0663 Ellen Lindner, USA

0664   Terry Aske, Canada

0665   Wil Opio Oguta, Netherlands

0666   Marjolijn van Wijk, Netherlands

0667   Cindy Richard, Israel

0668 Melanie Grant, USA

0669 Ann Ribbens, USA

0670 Coleen Adderley, Canada

0671 Maya Schonenberger, USA

0672 Patricia Scott, Canada

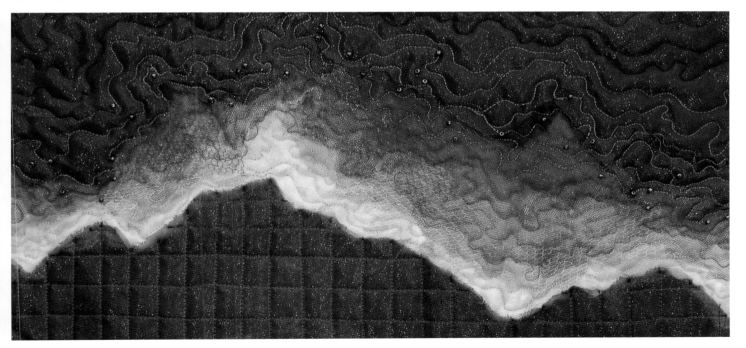

0673 Ellen Lindner, USA

0674   Hui-Fen Jessica Lin, Taiwan

0675   Miriam K. Sokoloff, USA

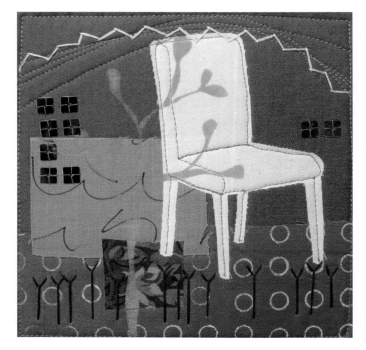

0676   Deborah Boschert, USA

0677   Elaine Millar, USA

0678 Marjorie Post, USA

0679 Carol Seeley, Canada

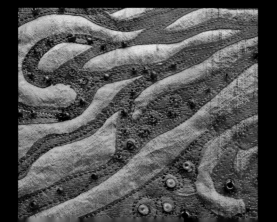

Abstract and Conceptual
Art Quilt Designs

CHAPTER 4

0680-0970

0680   Charity McAllister, USA

0681   Therese May, USA

0682   Therese May, USA

0683   Therese May, USA

0685   Wen Redmond, USA

0686   Wen Redmond, USA

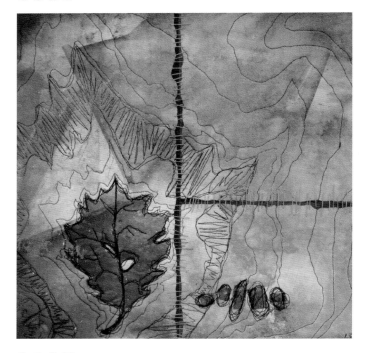

0687   Wen Redmond, USA

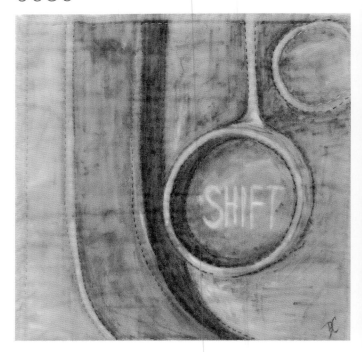

0688   Barbara Chapman, Canada

0689   Wen Redmond, USA

0690 Deborah Boschert, USA

0691 K. Velis Turan, USA

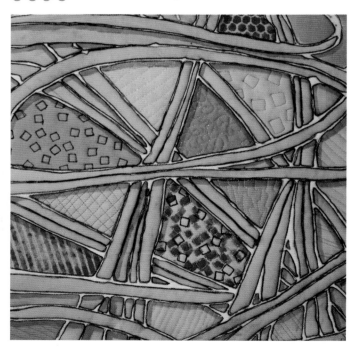

0692 K. Velis Turan, USA

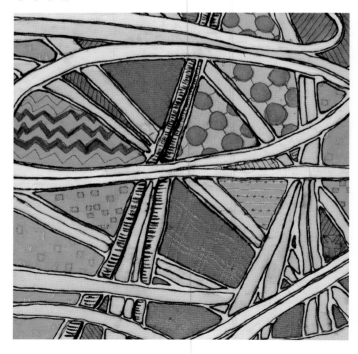

0693 K. Velis Turan, USA

0694 Dianne Firth, Australia

0695 Dianne Firth, Australia

0696 Carolynn McMillan, Canada

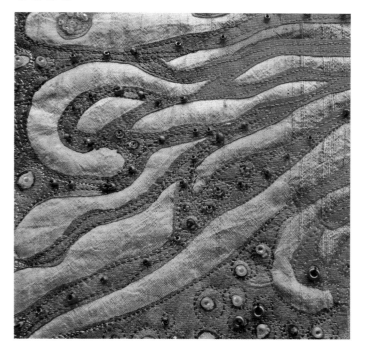

0697 Carolynn McMillan, Canada

0698 Brenda Gael Smith, Australia

0699 Brenda Gael Smith, Australia

0700 Heather Pregger, USA

0701 Heather Pregger, USA

0702　Julie R. Filatoff, USA

0703　Karen Farmer, UK

0704　Heather Pregger, USA

0705　Heather Pregger, USA

NARRATIVE VOICE

CHARACTERIZATION

SETTING

"Although it's true
I'm pretty clever,
and I'm something
of a rascal,
but all that's
well hidden under
this always easy
and natural disguise
of behaving like a fool."

Don Quixote

0706   David Charity, USA

0707   Lin Hsin-Chen, Taiwan

0708   Denise Oyama Miller, USA

0709   Jin-Gook Yang,
South Korea

0710   Diane Becka, USA

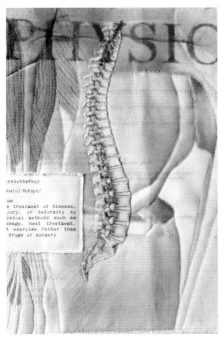

0711   Georgina Newson, UK

0712 Sue Benner, USA

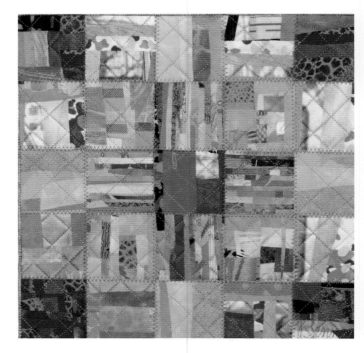

0713 Sue Benner, USA

0714 Sue Benner, USA

0715 Sue Benner, USA

0716 Kathie Briggs, USA

0717 Kathie Briggs, USA

0718 Kathie Briggs, USA

0719 Cynthia H. Catlin, USA

0720 Tafi Brown, USA

0721 Tafi Brown, USA

0722 Tafi Brown, USA

0723 Tafi Brown, USA

0724   Tafi Brown, USA

0725   Tafi Brown, USA

0726   Tafi Brown, USA

0727   Judy Paschalis, USA

Abstract and Conceptual Art Quilt Designs

221

0728 Jeannie Palmer Moore, USA

0729 Jamie Fingal, USA

0730 Robin DeMuth Schofield, USA

0731 Rhonda Baldwin, USA

0732 Marianne R. Williamson, USA

0733 Linda Kittmer, Canada

0734 Linda Kittmer, Canada

0735 Valya, USA

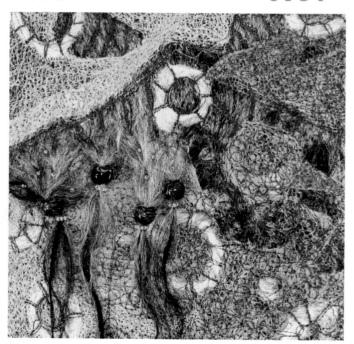

0736 Linda Kittmer, Canada

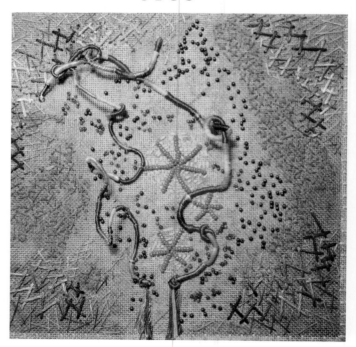

0737 Linda Kittmer, Canada

0738 Lyric Montgomery Kinard, USA

0739 Rose Rushbrooke, USA

0740 Michele Sanandajian, USA

0741   Michele Sanandajian, USA

0742   Joan Dyer, USA

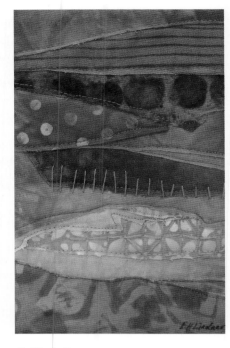

0743   Ellen Lindner, USA

0744   Virginia A. Spiegel, USA

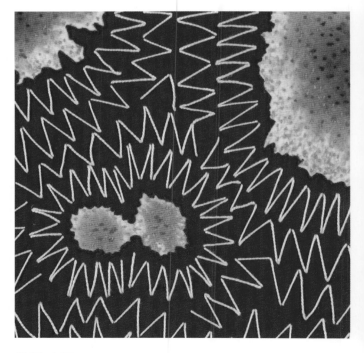

0745   Barbara W. Watler, USA

0746 Barbara W. Watler, USA

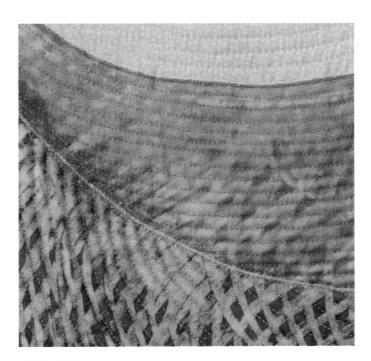

0747 Barbara W. Watler, USA

0748 Vivian Kapusta, Canada

0749 Julie Duschack, USA

0750 Belinda Hart, USA

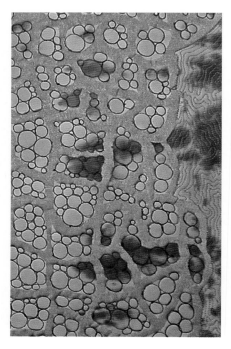

0751 Belinda Hart, USA

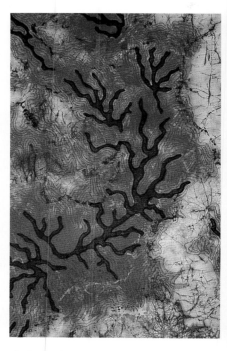

0752 Belinda Hart, USA

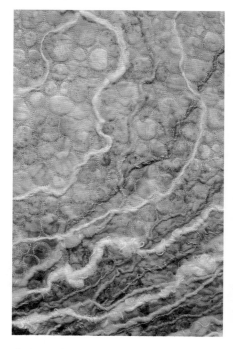

0753 Carolyn Carson, USA

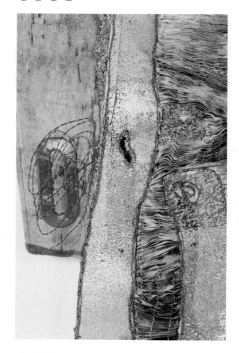

0754 Sue Hotchkis, UK

0755 Sue Hotchkis, UK

0756   Sue Hotchkis, UK

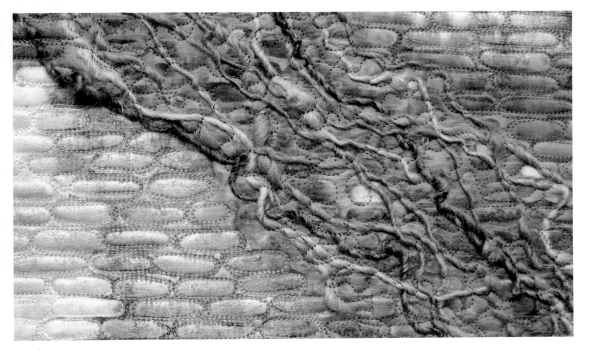

0757   Carolyn Carson, USA

0758 Carol Larson, USA

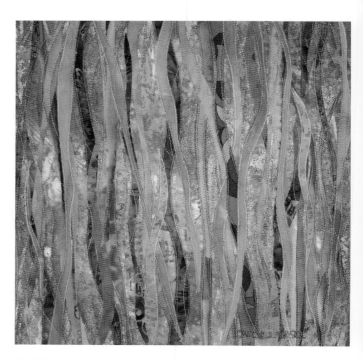

0759 Carol Larson, USA

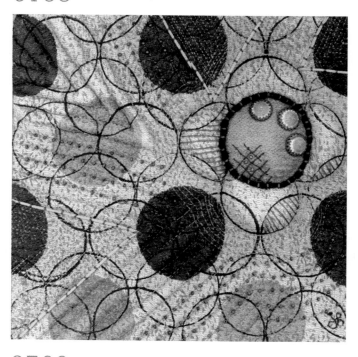

0760 Jennifer Hammond Landau, USA

0761 Karen Markley, USA

0762   Nancy Dobson, USA

0763   Carolynn McMillan, Canada

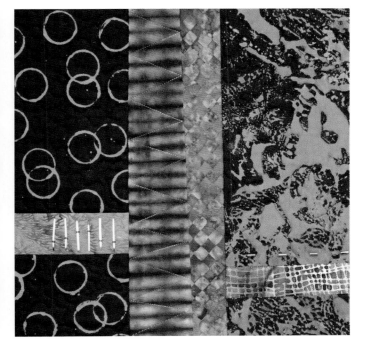

0764   Shelly Burge, USA

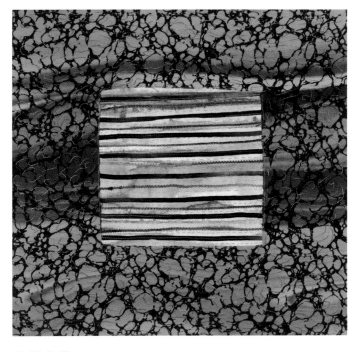

0765   Clairan Ferrono, USA

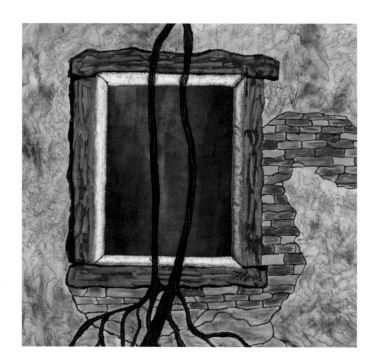

0766 Patricia Gould, USA

0767 Charity McAllister, USA

0768 Annie Helmericks-Louder, USA

0769 Annie Helmericks-Louder, USA

0770　Ann Grundler, USA

0771　Ann Grundler, USA

0772　Ann Grundler, USA

0773　Ann Grundler, USA

0774　Ann Grundler, USA

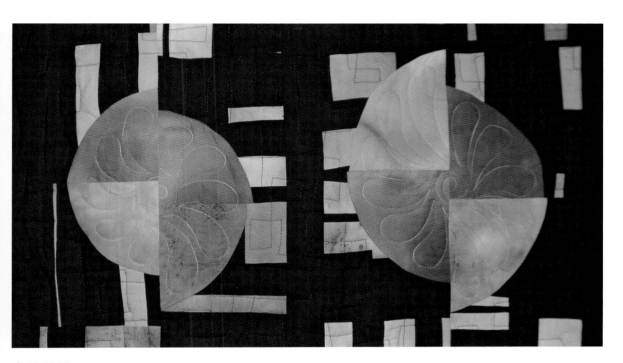

0775 Helene Kusnitz, USA

0776 Katharina Litchman, USA

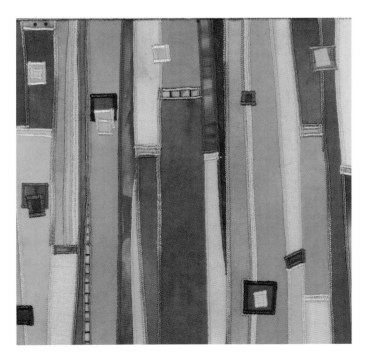

0777 Anne Solomon, Canada

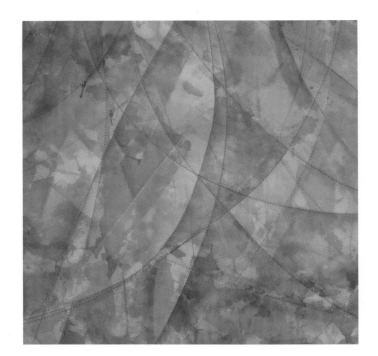

0778   Nelda Warkentin, USA

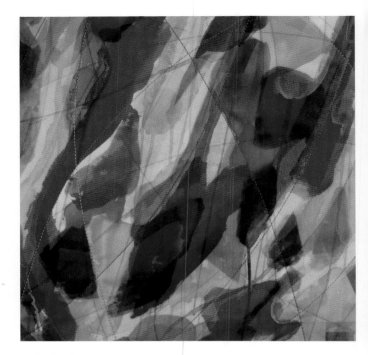

0779   Nelda Warkentin, USA

0780   Diane Eastham, Canada

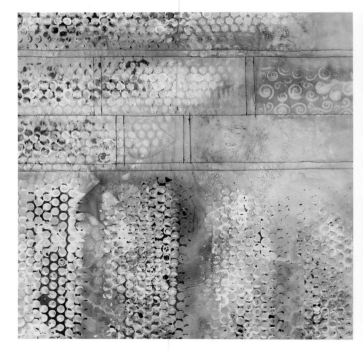

0781   Diane Eastham, Canada

0782   Lisa Corson, USA

0783   Lyric Montgomery Kinard, USA

0784   Lyric Montgomery Kinard, USA

0785   Lyric Montgomery Kinard, USA

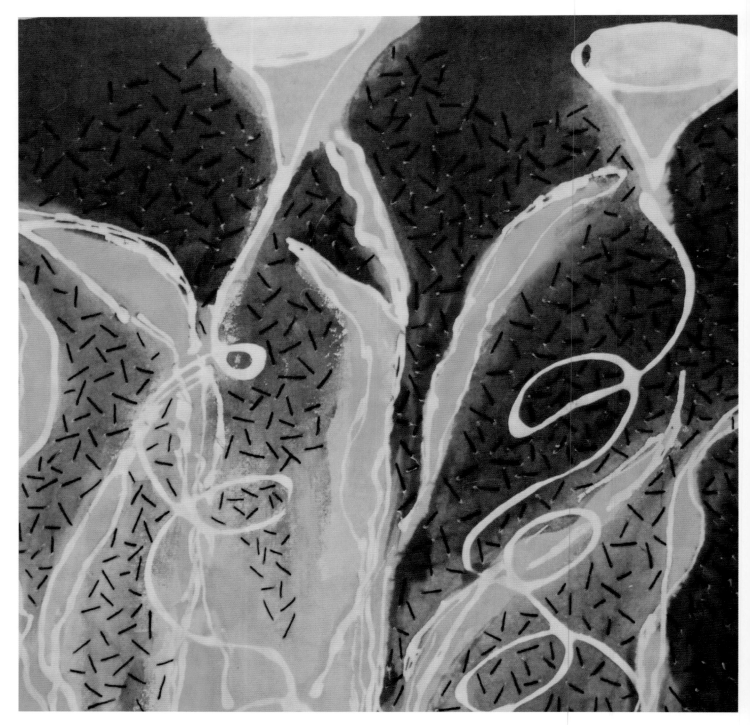

0786   Colleen Ansbaugh, USA

0787   Marijke van Welzen, Netherlands

0788   Virginia A. Spiegel, USA

0789   Colleen Ansbaugh, USA

0790   Carol Larson, USA

0791   Shelley Brucar, USA

0792 Marianne Burr, USA

0793 Marianne Burr, USA

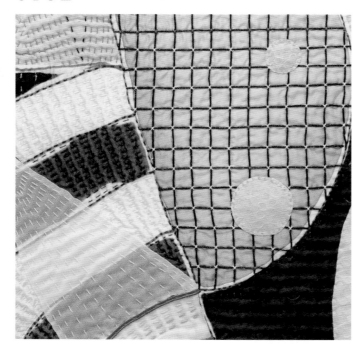

0794 Marianne Burr, USA

0795 Marianne Burr, USA

0796   Marianne Burr, USA

0797   Julie R. Filatoff, USA

0798   Gail P. Sims, USA

0799   Gail P. Sims, USA

0800   Mary T. Buchanan, USA

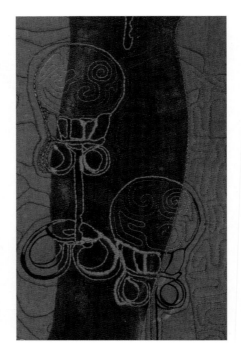

0801   Mary T. Buchanan, USA

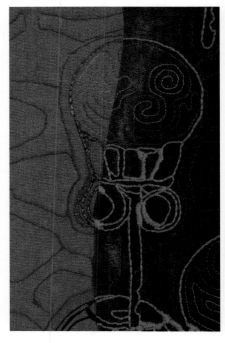

0802   Mary T. Buchanan, USA

0803   Kimberly Lapacek, USA

0804   Julie Duschack, USA

1000 QUILT INSPIRATIONS

0805 Carole Ann Frocillo, USA

0806 Anna Gajewska, Canada

0807 Pat Kroth, USA

0808 Pat Kroth, USA

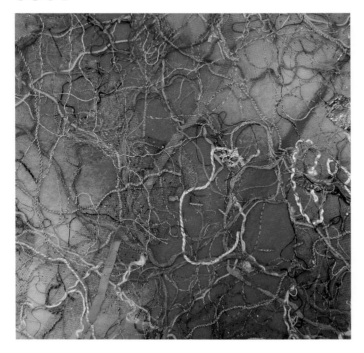

0809 Pat Kroth, USA

0810 Britta Ankenbauer, Germany

0811 Carol Larson, USA

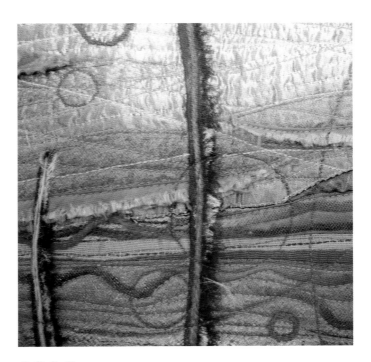

0812 Anna Gajewska, Canada

0813 Pat Kroth, USA

0814 Mary Markworth, USA

0815 Vita Marie Lovett, USA

0816 Vita Marie Lovett, USA

0817 Judith Mundwiler,
Switzerland

0818 Vita Marie Lovett, USA

0819 Karen Illman Miller, USA

0820 Ellen November, USA

0821   Randy Frost, USA

0822   Sheila Frampton-Cooper, USA

0823   Sheila Frampton-Cooper, USA

0824   Sheila Frampton-Cooper, USA

0825 Katie Pasquini Masopust, USA

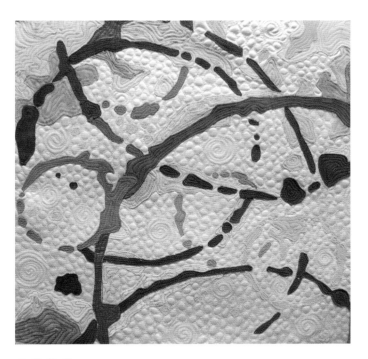

0826 Katie Pasquini Masopust, USA

0827 Linda Kittmer, Canada

0828 Linda Kittmer, Canada

0829   Ellen Lindner, USA

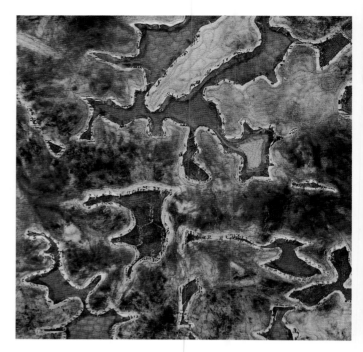

0830   Jana Sterbova, Czech Republic

0831   Valya, USA

0832   Ellen Lindner, USA

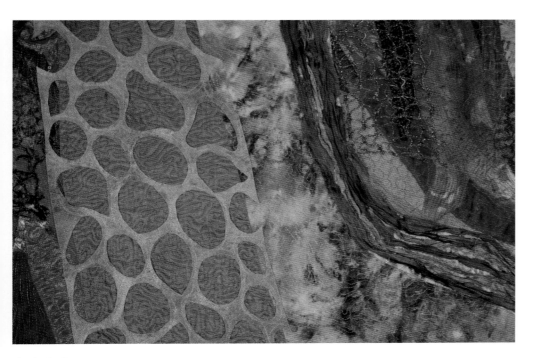

0833   Jana Sterbova, Czech Republic

0834   Jana Sterbova, Czech Republic

0835   Michele Sanandajian, USA

0836   Michele Sanandajian, USA

0837   Michele Sanandajian, USA

0838   Katie Pasquini Masopust, USA

0840   Colleen Ansbaugh, USA

0841   Nancy Billings, USA

0842   Wil Opio Oguta, Netherlands

0843   Nancy Billings, USA

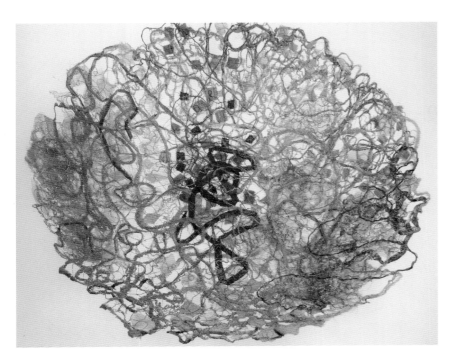

0844   Pat Hertzberg, Canada

0845   Janice Paine-Dawes, USA

0846 Joy Nebo Lavrencik, USA

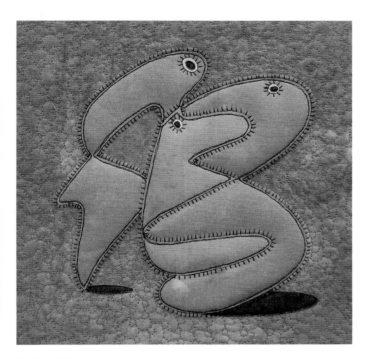

0847 Dahlia Clark, Canada

0848 Dahlia Clark, Canada

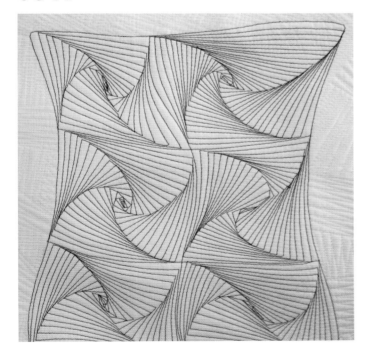

0849 Julie Snow, USA

0850 Bob Mosier, USA

0851   Diane Eastham, Canada

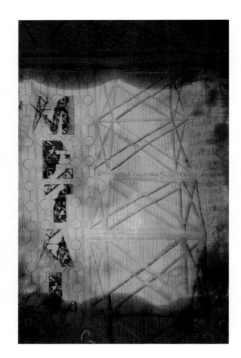

0852   Chris Dixon, UK

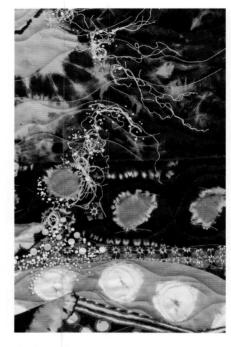

0853   Randy Frost, USA

0854   Barbara W. Watler, USA

0855   Christine Seager, UK

0856 Patricia Malarcher, USA

0857 Patricia Malarcher, USA

0858 Camilla Brent Pearce, USA

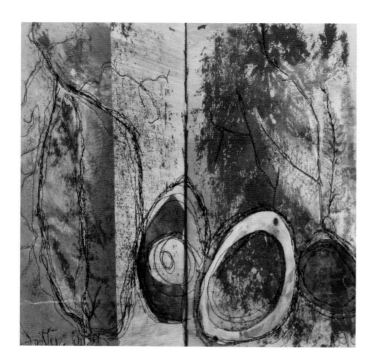

0859   Wen Redmond, USA

0860   Wen Redmond, USA

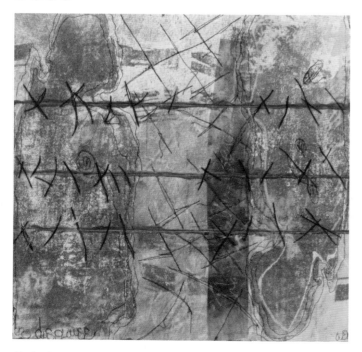

0861   Wen Redmond, USA

0862   Meg Cowey, Australia

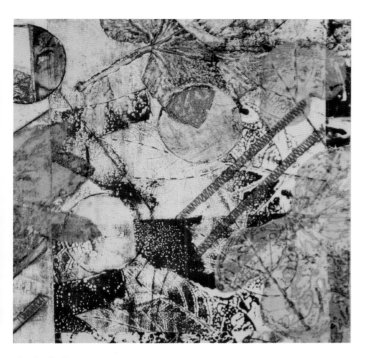

0863 Dominie Nash, USA

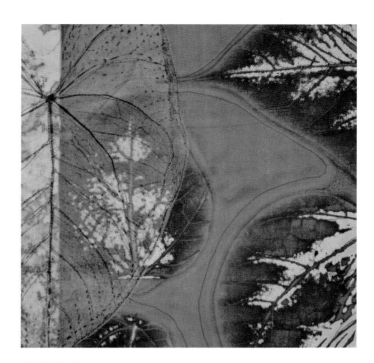

0864 Dominie Nash, USA

0865 Judith Mundwiler, Switzerland

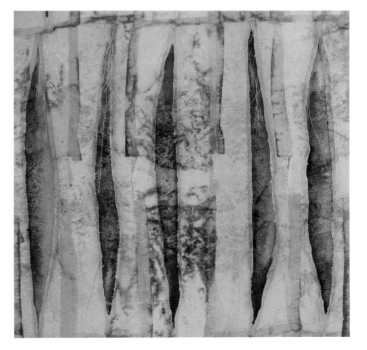

0866 Judith Mundwiler, Switzerland

0867 Nancy Bardach, USA

0868 Margaret (Meg) Filiatrault, USA

0869 Corinne Zambeek-van Hasselt, Netherlands

0870 Joanne Alberda, USA

0871   Wendy Read, USA

0872   Anna Gajewska, Canada

0873   Anna Gajewska, Canada

0874   Dianne Browning, USA

0875   Miriam Basart, USA

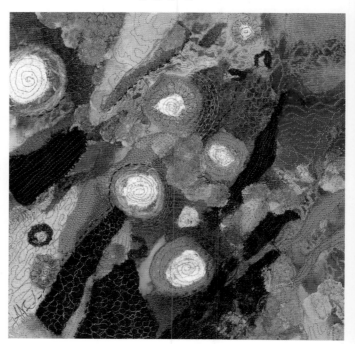

0876   Jeanelle McCall, USA

0877   Marjorie Post, USA

0878   Marjorie Post, USA

0879   Odette Tolksdorf, South Africa

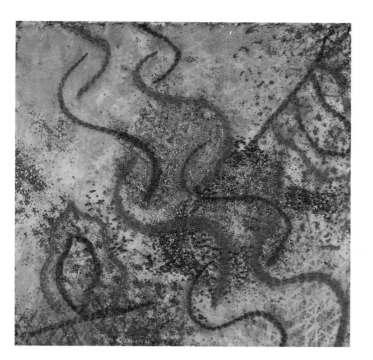

0880   Jeri C. Pollock, USA

0881   Jeri C. Pollock, USA

0882   Randy Frost, USA

0883   Britta Ankenbauer, Germany

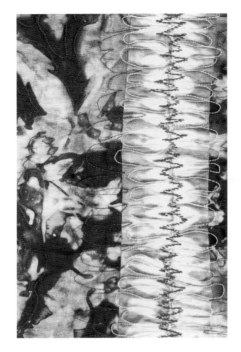

0884   Gail P. Sims, USA

0885   Holly Altman, USA

0886   Holly Altman, USA

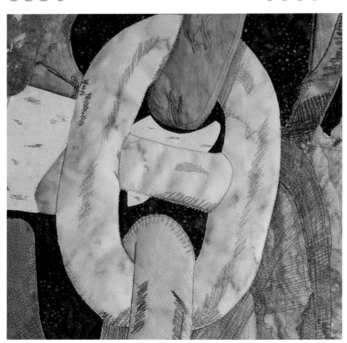

0887   Sharon Wiley Hightower, USA

0888   Judy Doolan Kjellin, Sweden

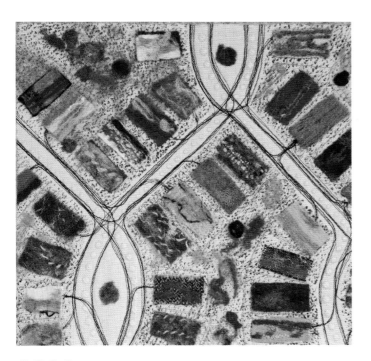

0889 Jennifer Hammond Landau, USA

0890 Jennifer Hammond Landau, USA

0891 Jean Wells Keenan, USA

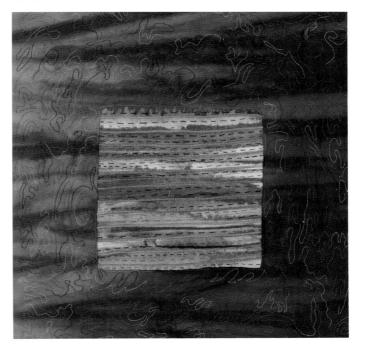

0892 Clairan Ferrono, USA

0893 Randy Frost, USA

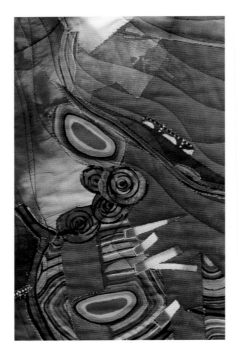

0894 Randy Frost, USA

0895 Randy Frost, USA

0896 Nancy Dobson, USA

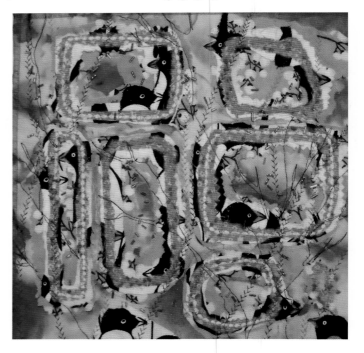

0897 Sharon Buck, USA

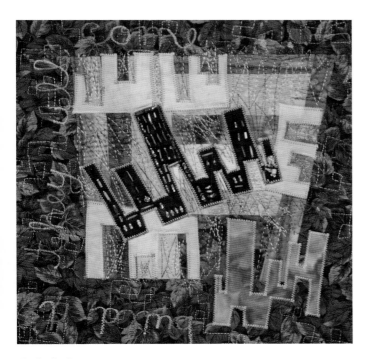

0898   Patricia Scott, Canada

0899   LaVerne Kemp, USA

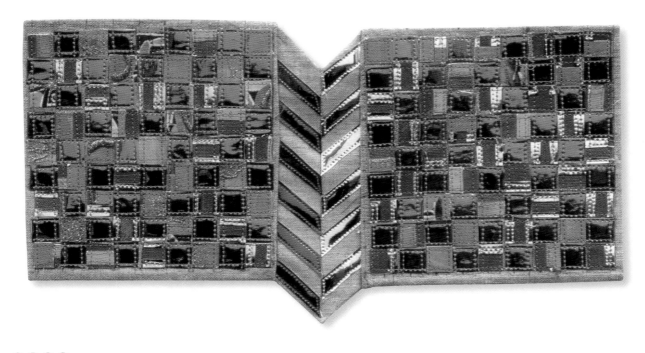

0900   Patricia Malarcher, USA

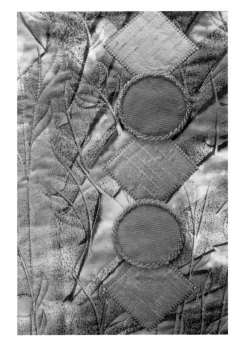

0901   Robbie Payne, USA

0902   Vivian Kapusta, Canada

0903   Enid Viljoen, South Africa

0904   Enid Viljoen, South Africa

0905   Carole Ann Frocillo, USA

0906   Lisa Corson, USA

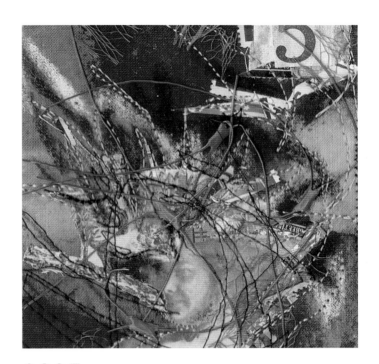

0907   Lisa Corson, USA

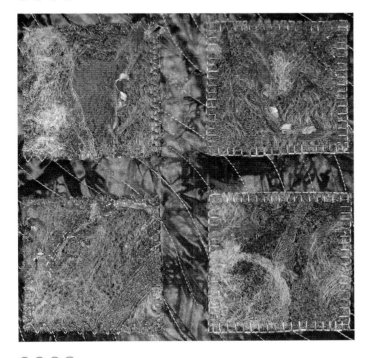

0908   Julie R. Filatoff, USA

0909   Naomi S. Adams, USA

0910　Natalie Isvarin-Love, USA

0911　Gwendolyn Aqui-Brooks, USA

0912　Linda Kittmer, Canada

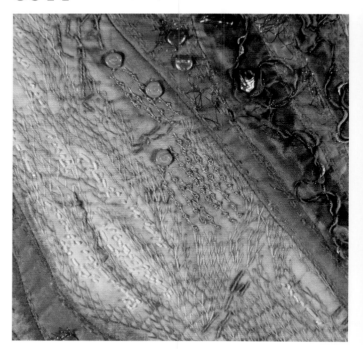

0913　Jeri C. Pollock, USA

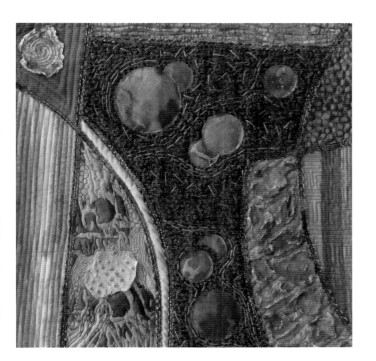

0914 David Charity, USA

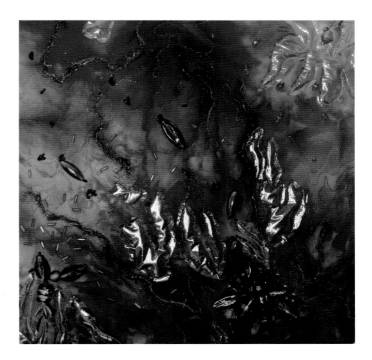

0915 Susan Wittrup, Canada

0916 Heidi Zielinski, USA

0917 Arle Sklar-Weinstein, USA

0918   Sharon Casey, USA

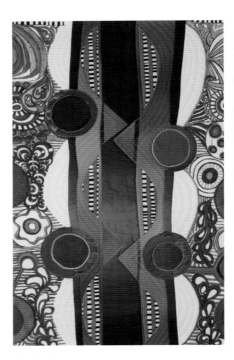

0919   Sharon Casey, USA

0920   Valya, USA

0921   Valya, USA

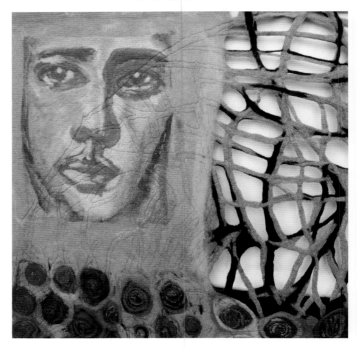

0922   Valya, USA

0923 Bethany E. Garner, Canada

0924 Mary Markworth, USA

0925 Heidi Zielinski, USA

0926 Gail P. Sims, USA

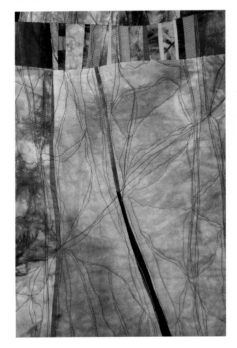

0927 Jean Wells Keenan, USA

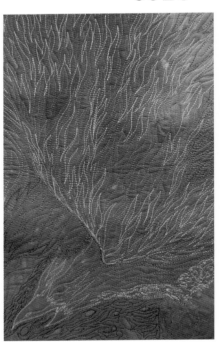

0928 Sion Thomas, Australia

0929 Amie Starchuk, Saudi Arabia

0930 Holly Altman, USA

0931 Elizabeth Barton, USA

0932 Sue Hotchkis, UK

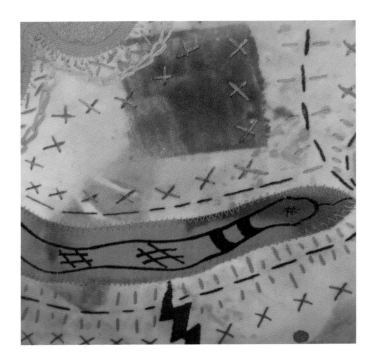

0933 Judy Cobillas, USA

0934 Amie Starchuk, Saudi Arabia

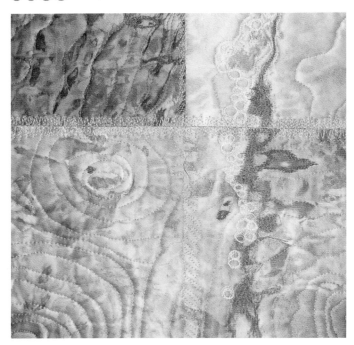

0935 Charlotte Ziebarth, USA

0936 Anne Solomon, Canada

0937   Gunnel Hag, Canada

0938 Hope Wilmarth, USA

0939 Shirley Mooney, New Zealand

0940 Ann Grundler, USA

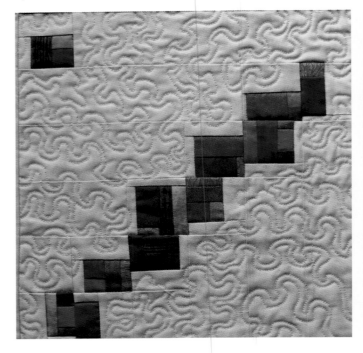

0941 Patricia Forster, Australia

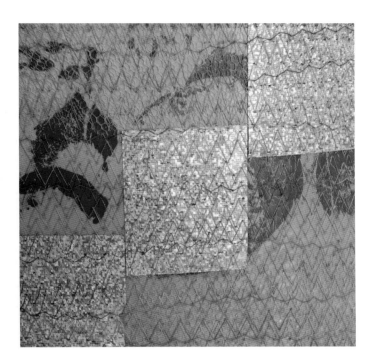

0942 Arturo Alonto Sandoval, USA

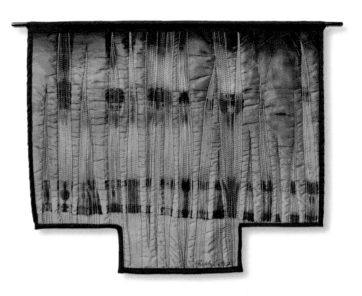

0943 Judith Content, USA

0944 Hui-Fen Jessica Lin, Taiwan

0945 Arturo Alonzo Sandoval, USA

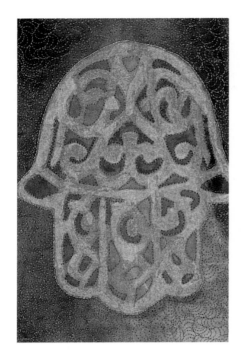

0946 Amie Starchuk,
Saudi Arabia

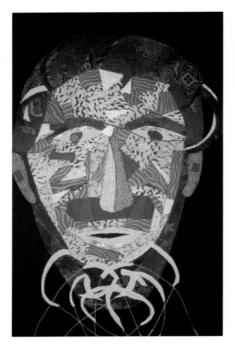

0947 Cuauhtemoc Q Kish, USA

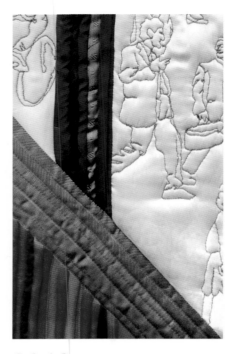

0948 Brigitte Kopp, Germany

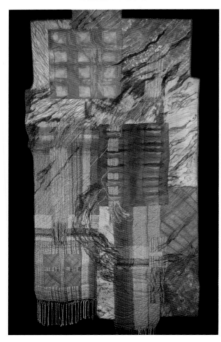

0949 Roseline Young, USA

0950 Pat Bishop, USA

0951 Elizabeth Barton, USA

0952   Arturo Alonzo Sandoval, USA

0954   Mary Markworth, USA

0953   Britta Ankenbauer, Germany

0955 Jana Lalova, Czech Republic

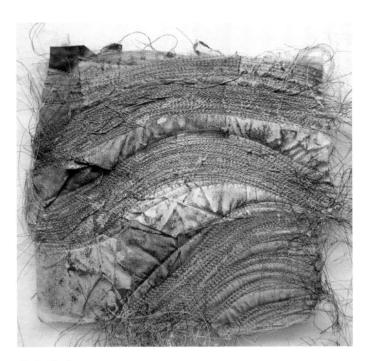

0956 Nancy Billings, USA

0957 Nancy Billings, USA

0958 Nancy Billings, USA

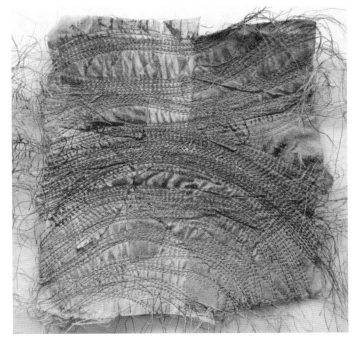

0959 Nancy Billings, USA

0960   Shea Wilkinson, USA

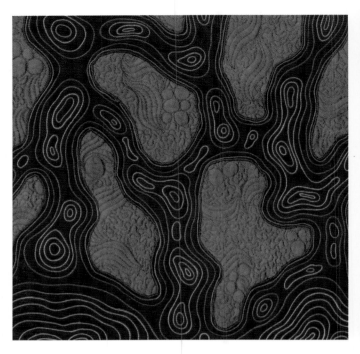

0961   Shea Wilkinson, USA

0962   Dianne Firth, Australia

0963   Nelda Warkentin, USA

0964 Arturo Alonzo Sandoval, USA

0965 Arturo Alonzo Sandoval, USA

0966 Elizabeth Barton, USA

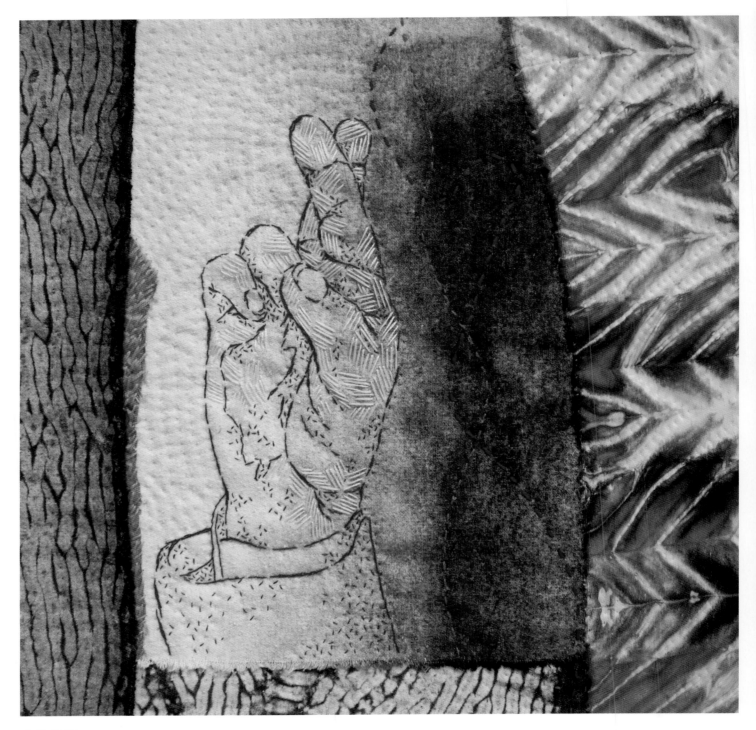

0967 Elizabeth Fram, USA

0968   Elizabeth Barton, USA

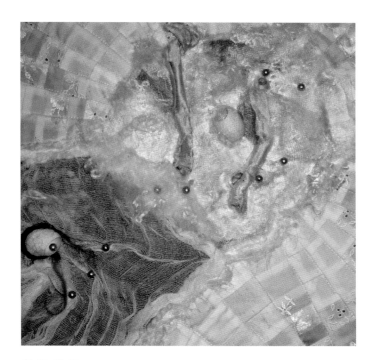

0969   Jana Lalova, Czech Republic

0970   Cynthia Stentz, USA

About the Author and Her Quilts

Dr. Sandra Sider, a New York–studio quilt artist, has published articles and reviews concerning fiber art and other aspects of visual culture for three decades. Her graduate degrees include an M.A. in art history from the Institute of Fine Arts, New York University. She is a past president of Studio Art Quilt Associates and curator for the Texas Quilt Museum. Sider's quilts are in the collections of museums, hospitals, and the Hartsfield-Jackson Atlanta International Airport, and have been selected for numerous juried exhibitions. She has specialized in photographic processes since 1980. See more of her work at www.sandrasider.com.

0971 Fanfare #2, Floating Lotus

0972 3 x 3 #1, Cactus (New York)

0973   Garden Grid #3

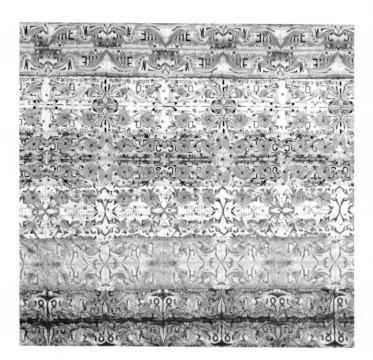

0974   On the Road, Curves Ahead

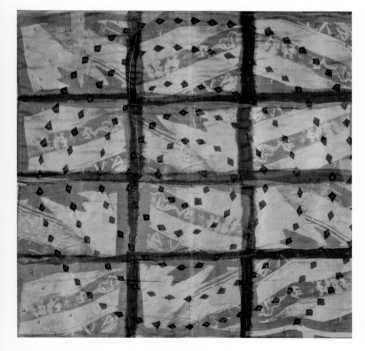

0975   Penumbra #8, Love Letters

0976   Tutti Frutti (detail)

0977 Garden Grid #5 (detail)

0978 Garden Grid #5

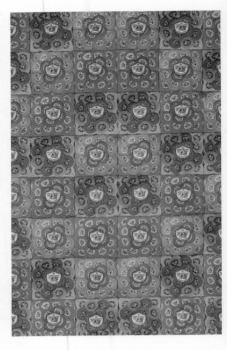

0979 Tutti Frutti

0980 On the Road,
Curves Ahead, detail

0981 Going Home

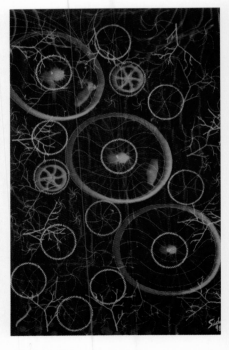

0982 Water Wheels

0983   Garden Grid #2 (detail)

0984   Garden Grid #3 (detail)

0985   Penumbra #7, Twilight

0986   Penumbra #7, Twilight (detail)

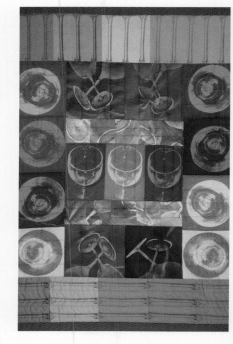

0987   Bottoms Up!

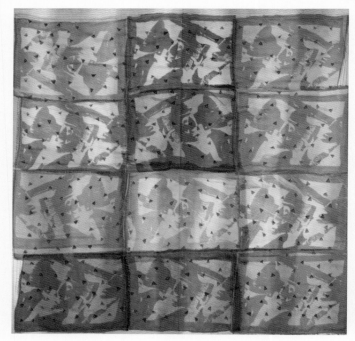

0988   Penumbra #2, Silent Soldiers

0989   Penumbra #3, Rule of Silence

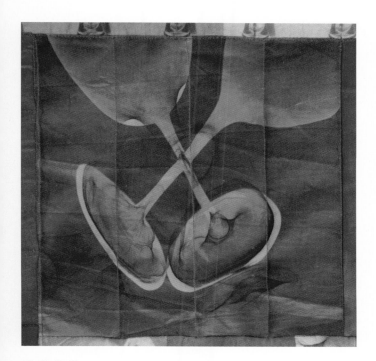

0990   Bottoms Up! (detail)

0991   Women at Work and Play #7

0992   Penumbra #4, Reliquary

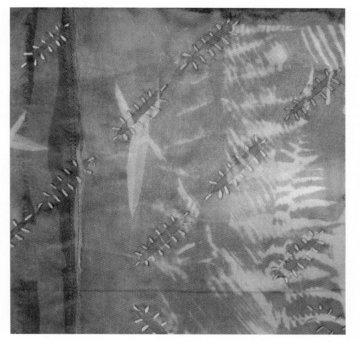

0993   Penumbra #4, Reliquary (detail)

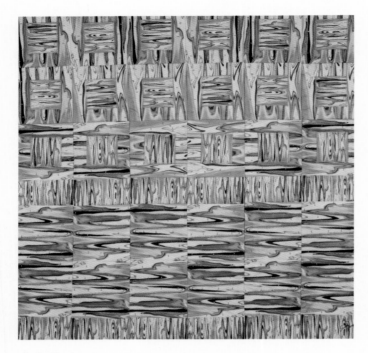

0994   On the Road, Slippery When Wet

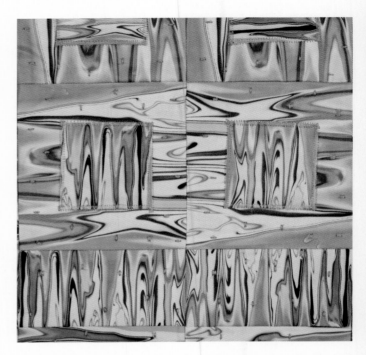

0995   On the Road, Slippery When Wet (detail)

0996   On the Road, Road Rage

0997   On the Road, Road Rage (detail)

0998   **Boogie-Down Kitchen**

0999   **Chapultepec Flash**

1000   **Knight Watch**

Image Directory

Chapter 1

0001 *Block Filmstrip* (block) **0002** *Block Filmstrip* (block) **0003** *Block Filmstrip* (block) **0004** *Block Filmstrip* (block) **0005** Commercial cottons **0006** Commercial fabrics **0007** Commercial fabrics **0008** Commercial fabrics **0009** *Eye See What's on Your Plate* (Kaleidoscope block) **0010** Machine-quilted **0011** Machine-quilted **0012** Machine-quilted **0013** *Kansas City Star* (sampler), miniature, reproduction fabrics **0014** Machine-quilted **0015** *Sawtooth Star Block* **0016** Hand-dyed fabric **0017** *Alabama State Quilt* (sampler) **0018** *It's the Little Things That Count*, miniature quilt blocks, Pineapple Log Cabin blocks, batiks **0019** *Off the Grid*, 18″x 18″ (45.7 x 45.7 cm), commercial cottons, machine-pieced and machine-quilted **0020** *It's Hip To Be Square*, 18″x 18″ (45.7 x 45.7 cm), commercial cottons, machine-pieced and machine-quilted **0021** Traditional pieced quilt **0022** Untitled detail, traditional costume fabric from Spakenburg; piecing **0023** Machine-quilted **0024** *Angst*, miniature, second of a series of three quilts, scraps, embellished with beads and fibers **0025** This project received first place in a competition. **0026** Longarm quilted **0027** Jo Morton star pattern and fabric **0028** *I Love Baskets*, blue-and-white basket blocks **0029** *A Feathered Star* (unfinished), paper-piece technique **0030** *A Star in a Star* (block) 12″ x 12″ (30.5 x 30.5 cm), traditional block, free-motion quilted **0031** *Feathered Rose* **0032** *Ten Minute Block*, stitched and stuffed **0033** *Flowers and Butter-flies* (detail) **0034** *Flowers and Butterflies* (detail) **0035** *Flower Parade Brown*, 22″ x 23″ (56 x 58.4 cm), traditional costume fabric from Spakenburg, raw-edge appliquéd, free-motion, machine-quilted **0036** *Flower Parade Purple*, 17″ x 22″ (43.2 x 56 cm), traditional costume fabric from Spaken-burg; raw-edge appliquéd, free-motion, machine-quilted **0037** *Mandala in Purple*, 22″ x 22″ (56 x 56 cm) batik fabrics, rhinestones, beads, machine-appliquéd, quilted **0038** *Mandala in Pink*, 22″ x 22″ (56 x 56 cm) batik fabrics, rhinestones, beads, machine-appliquéd, quilted **0039** Traditional mixed techniques **0040** Traditional mixed techniques **0041** *Fantastic* **0042** *Tangled Web* **0043** *Ma, How Come She Gets All the Attention?* **0044** *T-Carnival*, cotton, hand-dyed and Japanese antique fabric; reversible Log Cabin piecing; photo: D. James Dee **0045** *Heavenly Brilliance*, cotton, hand-dyed and Japanese antique fabric; machine-pieced, hand-appliquéd, hand-quilted; photo: D. James Dee **0046** *Smile*, cotton, commercial, hand-dyed, hand-painted, vintage silk, beads; machine pieced, hand-quilted, and embroidered; photo: D. James Dee **0047** Whole cloth quilt design printed on fabric,

8″ x 8″ (20.3 x 20.3 cm), fabric markers. Embellished with decorative stitches **0048** *Side Stepping*, 12″x 12″ (30.5 x 30.5 cm), commercial cottons, folded log cabin construction, machine-pieced and machine-quilted **0049** *Text Me*, 14″ x 14″ (35.6 x 35.6 cm) commercial cottons, folded log cabin construction, machine-pieced and machine-quilted **0050** Traditional block from a Dear Jane, traditional Dutch costume fabrics **0051** Traditional block from a Dear Jane, traditional Dutch costume fabrics **0052** *Broken Dishes* **0053** Raw-edge appliquéd, thread sketching **0054** *Modern Mini 2* **0055** *A Study of Black and White*, hand-stitched, beaded **0056** *Inspiration* **0057** *Laurel Wreath* (detail), block developed in Sally Schneider workshop, quilting by Shawna Crawford **0058** *Scrappy Baskets*, block quilt **0059** *Scrappy Baskets*, block quilt **0060** *Scrappy Baskets*, block quilt **0061** *Chicken Feathers* **0062** Traditional mixed techniques **0063** Crazy-quilt block, Dia de los Muertos (Day of the Dead) fabric; center fabric, fussy-cut, embellished with decorative stitch **0064** Crazy-quilt block, *Dia de los Muertos* (Day of the Dead) fabric; center fabric, fussy-cut, embellished with decorative stitch **0065** Crazy-quilt block, *Dia de los Muertos* (Day of the Dead) fabric; center fabric, fussy-cut, embellished with decorative stitch **0066** Crazy-quilt block, *Dia de los Muertos* (Day of the Dead) fabric; center fabric, fussy-cut, embellished with decorative stitch **0067** Crazy-quilt block, *Dia de los Muertos* (Day of the Dead) fabric; center fabric, fussy-cut, embellished with decorative stitch **0068** Crazy-quilt block, *Dia de los Muertos* (Day of the Dead) fabric; center fabric, fussy-cut, embellished with decorative stitch **0069** Crazy-quilt block, *Dia de los Muertos* (Day of the Dead) fabric; center fabric, fussy-cut, embellished with decorative stitch **0070** Japanese fabrics, embellished with prairie points **0071** *Gewitterhimmel* (Thunderstorm) **0072** *Goldenes Vlies* (Golden fleece) **0073** *Wirbelwind* (Twister) **0074** *Gluewuermchen* (Firefly) **0075** Coffee table runner with shooting stars, 16″ x 16 ″ (40.6 x 40.6 cm) cotton, machine-pieced and quilted **0076** Pattern strip star given a modern spin. Four-block setting. **0077** Batiks **0078** *Storm at Sea* **0079** *Windows*, 13″ x 13″ (33 x 33 cm), machine-pieced and quilted, cotton fabrics, batting **0080** Untitled detail, hand-dyed cotton, shibori, stitched **0081** *Splash*, 12″ x 16″ (30.5 x 40.6 cm), hand-dyed cotton, pleated, stitched **0082** *Drunkard's Path* **0083** *Megan's Quilt* (one block), prom gowns and pins **0084** *Bronze Elegance* (embel-lished crazy quilt block) **0085** *Bronze Elegance* (embellished crazy quilt block) **0086** *Crazy for Vintage* block (1 of 9 parts), 9″ x 9″ (23 x 23 cm), silk ribbon, brocade, vintage fabric,

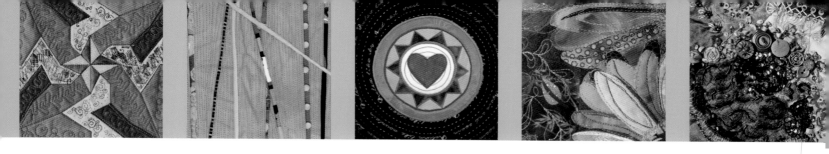

beads, French metallic thread, hand-dyed rayon motifs; silk ribbon embroidery **0087** Traditional embellished quilt **0088** *Patchwork Embellished* **0089** *Guild's Opportunity* (detail), miniature, paper-pieced, traditional-pieced **0090** Batik jewel-tone fabrics **0091** Scrappy brights and reds, pineapple Log Cabin block **0092** Center star of Christmas quilt made of half-square triangles **0093** Four paper-pieced fan blocks, Dresden plate block with square center **0094** *Token Token*, game boards attached with wooden dominos and beads, machine-quilted **0095** Carol Doak star pattern, four paper-pieced blocks **0096** Carol Doak star pattern, four paper-pieced blocks **0097** *Star Hunter*, cotton, hand-dyed and Japanese antique fabric; reversible Log Cabin piecing; photo: D. James Dee **0098** Heavenly Brilliance, cotton, hand-dyed and Japanese antique fabric; machine-pieced, hand-appliquéd, hand-quilted; photo: D. James Dee **0099** *The Princess of Weaving II*, cotton, Japanese antique fabric,Thai silk, machine-pieced, hand-appliquéd, hand-quilted; photo: Kayoko Watanabe **0100** *The Princess of Weaving I*, cotton, Japanese antique, self-made, hand-dyed, Japanese antique obi silk, machine-pieced, hand-appliquéd, hand-quilted; photo: D. James Dee **0101** Traditional pieced **0102** *Kaleidoscope* **0103** *Kaleidoscope* **0104** Design from *Kaleidoscope* **0105** Design from *Kaleidoscope* **0106** Design from *Kaleidoscope* **0107** *My Album* (one block), machine-quilted by Susan Corbett **0108** From the book, *A Perfect Union* by Darlene Christopherson (one block), needle turn appliquéd, machine-quilted by Susan Corbett **0109** *Desert Star*, machine-quilted by Susan Corbett **0110** *Bird With a Nest* (one block), wool-appliquéd on Daiwabo yarn-dyed cotton **0111** *Nebraska Navy*, machine-pieced commercial fabrics; longarm-quilted by Colleen Noecker **0112** *Nebraska Navy*, machine-pieced commercial fabrics; longarm-quilted by Colleen Noecker **0113** Traditional mixed techniques **0114** *Lone Star* (quilt block) **0115** *Cathedral Windows* (block), machine pieced, hand-stitched, commercial cotton fabrics **0116** *A Rose Garden*, pattern of right-angled isosceles triangles **0117** Work in progress, hand-dyed cotton, pieced, machine embroidered **0118** Traditional *Kaleidoscope* (quilt block) **0119** *Double T* **0120** *Memories from a Distant Sky*, cotton; machine-pieced and quilted **0121** *Chrysanthemum* (variation), batik fabrics, hand-quilted **0122** *Twelve Squared*, 12" X 12" (30.5 x 30.5 cm), silk and cotton batik, 5.5" (14 cm) squares, 144 half-square triangles in pink , lavender, and purple; photo: John Sims **0123** *Iris in Basket*, needle-turn appliqué, 15" (38 cm) **0124** *Sunrise Flutterby* (section of 26" X 40" [66 x 101.6 cm]) needle-turned appliqué, hand-quilted **0125**

Something To Crow About, hand-dyed cotton fabrics, machine-pieced and quilted **0126** *Grandmother's Jewels* **0127** 5 = 2 x 4 (The title refers to 5-inch [12.7 cm] square units), an original block sewn with vintage fabrics **0128** Traditional mixed techniques **0129** *Bluetenkranz* **0130** *Solar Flare*, resisted rust on cotton hand-marble dyed fabric, glass beads, copper foil, silk thread, hand-dyed cotton embroidery floss, and nylon thread. Machine-quilted, hand- beaded, hand-embroidered, hand-appliquéd, bound in copper **0131** *Montana Lone Star Center* **0132** Traditional pieced **0133** Detail photo by Darren Takegami; Full shot photo from Houston Int'l Quilt Festival. **0134** Traditional mixed techniques **0135** *Pinwheel Party* block, cotton fabrics, foundation paper-pieced **0136** *Broken Dishes* **0137** *Obsession*, machine-pieced and quilted, cotton fabrics and batting, 10" x 10" (25.4 x 25.4 cm) **0138** *Nightlights*, 14" x 14" (35.6 x 35.6 cm), machine-pieced, appliquéd, machine-quilted **0139** *Blue Feathers*, 12" x 12" (30.5 x 30.5 cm), machine-pieced, hand-appliquéd machine-quilted **0140** *Jazz & Blues* (center), over-dyed with indigo, arashi shibori (pole wrapping) to create the stripes **0141** *From Sea to Shining Sea* (center), includes the lyrics to "America, the Beautiful." Center quilted with the eagle from the US quarter. **0142** Appliquéd, hand-dyed and commercial fabrics **0143** *Feathered Stars & Redwork*, c. 1900 **0144** *Star Spangled Banner*, c. 1860 **0145** *Scherenschnitte Quilt*, c. 1895 **0146** *Birds & Grapes Appliqué*, c. 1870 **0147** *Pine Tree*, c. 1880 **0148** *Rose of Sharon*, variation, c. 1860 **0149** *Pots of Flowers with Stars*, c. 1860 **0150** *North Carolina Lily with Sunflowers* **0151** *Single Irish Chain* **0152** *Ohio Star with Sawtooth Border*, c. 1880 **0153** *Pineapple Appliqué*, c. 1890; 2003 **0154** *Nine Patch Criss-Cross*, c. 1895 **0155** *Touching Stars*, c. 1865 **0156** *Silk Victorian Log Cabin*, c. 1890 **0157** *Pineapple Log Cabin*, c. 1890 **0158** *New York Beauty*, c. 1930 **0159** *Nine Patch* variation, 1920 **0160** *Lover's Knot*, c. 1940 **0161** *Sampler*, c. 1880; 2003 **0162** *Log Cabin with Star center* **0163** *Log Cabin, Courthouse Steps*, variation, c. 1890 **0164** *Spiderweb*, c. 1900 **0165** *Garden Maze with Shoo Fly*, c. 1870 **0166** *Contained Crazy Quilt*, c. 1850–1875 **0167** *Log Cabin with Ohio Stars*, c. 1900 **0168** *President's Medallion*, c. 1889 **0169** *Vase of Tulips*, c. 1930 **0170** *Hawaiian Floral Urns*, c. 1930 **0171** *Prairie Flower*, c. 1870 **0172** *Whig Rose* **0173** *Pine Tree*, c. 1930 **0174** *Hawaiian Appliqué*, white on green, c. 1930 **0175** *Floral Picket Fence*, c. 1930 **0176** *Flower Garden*, c. 1930 **0177** *Friendship Album*, (detail), possibly Mennonite (early-twentieth century) **0178** *Roman Stripe* (detail), (1940s) **0179** *Star of Bethlehem* (detail), Mennonite quilt (1920s) **0180** *Joseph's Coat* (detail), Mennonite quilt (early-twentieth century)

widths **0265** Circle quadrant motif, pieced with bands of bright colors in various widths **0266** Circle quadrant motif, pieced with bands of bright colors in various widths **0267** Paper pieced with cotton fabric, 9" x 6" (23 x 15.2 cm) embellished, stitched using rayon and polyester thread **0268** Contemporary pieced **0269** Raw-edge appliquéd **0270** Contemporary pieced **0271** *Rustic Leaves*, Photo: Nick Seager **0272** Contemporary pieced **0273** *It's Not Easy Being Green*, 12" x 12" (30.5 x 30.5 cm) **0274** Abstract **0275** *Opening Violets Machine* (detail), cotton, pieced and quilted **0276** *Dreamlines #6*, hand-dyed cotton, free-form–pieced, machine-quilted **0277** *Red Rover* **0278** *Jacks* **0279** *Flying Kites* **0280** *Fishes Fly*, fused fabric collage, hand-dyed and commercial cottons **0281** *"A" is for Beginnings*, fused fabric collage, cotton **0282** *Evergreen*, 12" x 12" (30.5 x 30.5 cm), hand-dyed cotton, free-form–pieced, machine-quilted **0283** *Bush Tucker Tracks*, 12" x 12" (30.5 x 30.5 cm) hand-dyed cotton, freeform pieced, machine-quilted **0284** *Desert Tracks*, hand-dyed cotton, free-form–pieced, machine-quilted **0285** *Colorado Autumn Blaze* (detail), silk, silk/cotton fabrics, machine-pieced and quilted, appliquéd **0286** *Colorado Autumn Blaze* (detail), silk, silk/cotton fabrics, machine-pieced and quilted, appliquéd **0287** *Colorado Autumn Blaze* (detail), silk, silk/cotton fabrics, machine-pieced and quilted, appliquéd **0288** *The Heart of the Matter* (detail) cotton and velvet, appliquéd, beaded, stitched **0289** *Zinnias and Trees* (detail), cotton, pieced and quilted **0290** *Push Me, Pull Me* (detail) cotton, machine pieced **0291** *Push Me, Pull Me* (detail) cotton, machine pieced **0292** *Woven Colors*, dyed cotton, hand-dyed trim, machine-quilted **0293** *Modern Log Cabin*, Ombre fabrics, machine-quilted by Marcia Wachuta **0294** Stenciled and printed with thickened dye **0295** *The Heart of Matter* **0296** *Rings*, 12" x 12" (30.5 x 30.5 cm), Kona fabrics, pearl cotton thread, machine-quilted **0297** *A Tangled Web*, 10" x 10" (25.4 x 25.4 cm), 100% cotton batik fabrics, 80/20 batting, silver thread, spider button, silver fly charm, seed beads, strip pieced by machine, machine- quilted and beaded **0298** *Falling Leaves*, cotton batiks, silks, machine-pieced, quilted **0299** *Writing on the Wall*, machine-pieced with feather stitch, machine-quilted, satin stitch binding **0300** *Log Cabin*, 24" x 24" (61 x 61 cm), batiks, 100% cotton **0301** *Coloring Outside the Lines*, cotton, silk, shibori dyed fabric, machine-appliquéd **0302** *Cobblestones*, 8" x 12" (20.3. x 30.5 cm) machine-pieced and quilted **0303** *Breathe*, 32" x 32" (82 x 82 cm) organza and cotton fabrics, pompoms, rings of sisal string, hand- and machine-stitched **0304** *Love Never Fails*, 16" x 15" (40.6 x 38 cm) batiks, archival ink, embroidery thread, strip-pieced, embellished with batik, beads, calligraphy **0305** *Tumbing E*, (detail), commercial and hand-dyed cotton, machine-pieced, hand-quilted; photo: Chris Baker **0306** *Reflections on K Street*, 8" x 8" (20.3 x 20.3 cm), appliquéd, free-motion, machine embroidered, quilted, Photo: PRS Assoc. Kensington, Maryland **0307** *Reimagined*, 8" x 8" (20.3 x 20.3 cm), appliquéd, free-motion, machine embroidered, quilted; Photo: PRS Assoc. Kensington, MD **0308** *Shapes 6*, hand-dyed fabrics; machine- and hand-pieced, machine-quilted and hand-stitched **0309** Art in Fiber **0310** Pick-Up Sticks series **0311** Deco, free-motion, machine-embroidered, Photo: PRS Assoc., Kensington, MD **0312** *Reconstructed Strangeness*, 12" x 12" (30.5 x 30.5 cm), silks, cotton canvas, free-motion, machine-embroidered, Photo: G R Staley Photography **0313** *Abstract* **0314** *Earth and Sea through Attic Windows*, 31" x 29.5" (78.7 x 75 cm) cotton, polyester batting, machine-pieced, hand-quilted **0315** *Black and White #3*, black-and-white fabric, satin-stiched and appliquéd **0316** *Black and White #2*, 13" x 13" (33 x 33 cm) black-and-white fabric, satin-stiched and appliquéd **0317** *Vortex* (detail), cotton, machine-pieced and quilted **0318** Contemporary pieced **0319** Hand-painted fabric, raw-edge appliquéd **0320** *Synchronicity*, developed in Photoshop, digitally printed and constructed **0321** *YoYo 8: Raining Cats and Dogs Heavily*, beaded **0322** Reverse appliquéd, hand-stitched **0323** *Zinnias*, raw-edge appliquéd, hand-dyed cottons, cotton commercial prints **0324** *The Staircase* (detail), hand-dyed cotton, fabrics pieced **0325** Embellished with yarn **0326** Beaded **0327** Machine-stitched **0328** 12" x 12" (30.5 x 30.5 cm) **0329** *Speed*, 8.25" x 11.75" (20.36 x 30 cm), screen-printed, stenciled shadow, machine-quilted **0330** *Choices*, 12" x 12" (30.5 x 30.5 cm) linen, textured cottons, stitched, beaded **0331** *In Orbit Material*, batik, machine- mounted on frame **0332** *Luna y Tierra: Amarillo y Azul (Moon and Earth: Yellow and Blue)*, hand-dyed cottons, linen, natural materials (indigo, madder, bois d'arc, turmeric, avocado), pieced in freeform, Drunkards Path variation, hand and-machine quilted **0334** *Ombre*, hand-dyed fabrics, shibori dyed fabrics, commercial ombre fabric, machine-pieced and quilted **0335** *Dreamlines #1*, hand-dyed cotton, free-form–pieced, machine-quilted **0336** *Tumbling E*, commercial and hand-dyed cotton, machine-pieced, hand-quilted by Inge Lailvaux **0337** *Flying Colors: Eclectus Parrots*, hand-dyed cotton, free-form–pieced, machine-quilted **0338** *Flying Colors: Crimson Rosella*, hand-dyed cotton, free-form–pieced, machine-quilted **0339** *Chartreuse is a Neutral* **0340** *Shadow Traces*, 23.5" x 29.5" (60 x 75 cm), organza, commercial and hand-dyed cotton, embroidery thread, hand and machine-stitched **0341** *Shadow Traces*, 23.5" x 29.5" (60 x 75 cm) organza and other sheer fabrics, commercial and hand-dyed cotton, embroidered, hand- and machine-stitched **0342** *Rock Houses* **0343** *Dimensional Rectangles* (detail), hand-painted silk, organza, embellished with copper rectangles, glass seed beads, hand-stitched, machine-quilted **0344** *Detail of Indigo*, dyed fabrics, vintage damask, red Japanese print fabric, machine-pieced, machine-quilted, hand-stitched pearl cotton thread **0345** *Treasures from the Old Loft* (detail), wool, hand- and machine-appliquéd **0346** *Pinwheel and Geese IV*, 13" x 13" (33 x 33 cm) hand-dyed cotton, cotton batting and backing, quilted with cotton thread, machine-pieced and machine-quilted **0347** *Still Breathing*, organza, cotton, and silk, pom-poms, rings of sisal string **0348** *Gum Nuts*, 12" x 12" (30.5 x 30.5 cm), hand-dyed and printed fabric, cotton, silk, velvet, hand-made stamp and thermofax screen, embossed **0349** *Units 31-Rhythm in Lights*, 36" x 36" (91.4 x 91.4 cm) cotton fabrics, fabric paints, cotton/poly batting, polyester thread; Machine-pieced and machine-quilted **0350** *Wonky Log Cabin Blue Patchwork*, limited edition, 27" x 25" (68.6 x 63.5 cm) , cotton, machine-pieced and quilted **0351** *Neon Tile #3* (detail), silk, black sheer, heat-distressed, machine-stitched **0352** *Hexagons*, cotton, hand-pieced, hand-dyed **0353** *Diatoms II*, hand-painted silk, painted Reme, oil sticks, machine-quilted **0354** *Tutu Flower*, 8" x 8" (20.3 x 20.3 cm) **0355** *Traditional Log Cabin* (quilt block) **0356** Bridges, dupioni silks, free-motion quilted with silk threads **0357** *Oxbows*, 8" x 10" (20.3 x 25.4 cm) cotton batiks, free-motion quilted **0358** *Iris* (detail), cotton, machine-pieced and quilted **0359** 14" (35.6 cm) abstract design **0360** *Bounded Enthusiasm* (detail), cotton, machine-pieced and quilted **0361** *Tequila Sunrise*, 12" x 12" (30.5 x 30.5 cm), collaged, layered and stitched with re-claimed sari silks **0362** *Surge* (detail), handmade silk paper, tulle, and foil, felted and stitched **0363** *Garden by the Sea* (detail), cotton, machine-pieced and quilted **0364** Contempo-rary mixed techniques **0365** Contemporary appliquéd **0366** *More and More Possibilities*, silk, cotton, machine-pieced and quilted **0367** *Tiny Dreams*, (detail) cotton fabrics, thread, embellishments, hand-quilted **0368** *Tic Toc* **0369** Abstract **0370** Abstract **0371** Photos: Andrew Pinkham **0372** Abstract **0373** *Art in Fiber* **0374** *Deep in the Heart* **0375** *Deep in the Heart* Its Art to Me, cotton, machine-appliquéd, quilted **0377** Three of a Kind, silk, cotton, machine-quilted **0378** *Study in Scraps*, 12" x 12" (30.5 x 30.5 cm), hand-dyed, bleach discharged, rust-printed, commercial fabrics **0379** *An Uphill Struggle*, 10" x 10" (25.4 x 25.4 cm), 100% cotton fabrics, 80/20 batting, fused machine appliquéd, machine quilted, satin stitched, hand-beaded **0380** *Study in Blue*, 12" x 12" (30.5 x 30.5 cm), hand-dyed, rust-printed, commercial fabric, quilted with gold metallic thread **0381** *Spiral of Absurdity*, 10" x 10" (25.4 x 25.4 cm), 100% cotton fabrics, 80/20 batting, seed beads, shell button, foundation pieced by machine, hand-quilt-ed and beaded **0382** *Ferns Within Grids*, machine, free-motion quilted, hand-stitched **0383** Hand-dyed and screen printed, appliquéd, embellished, machine-stitched and quilted **0384** *The Edge of Space* **0385** *Fireball Mini*, 12" x 12" (30.5 x 30.5 cm), hand-dyed cottons, oil paint sticks, raw-edge appliquéd, thread painting **0386** *Spiral Sphere*, 12" x 12" (30.5 x 30.5 cm), hand-dyed cottons, oil paint sticks, raw-edge appliquéd, thread painting **0387** Cotton, fused, machine-quilted **0388** *From Edge 2 Edge* **0389** *Notan with Leaves*, 9.5" x 11.5" (24 x 29 cm), dupioni silk, machine-pieced and appliquéd, machine-embroidered **0390** *Everything Will Be Fine*, 42" x 42" (106.6 x 106.6 cm) , cotton, viscose, mixed fibers, hand-appli-quéd, embroidered and quilted **0391** *Moon of Falling Leaves*, glass and stone beads, pearl cotton hand stitches, couched yarns, thread painted, commercial and hand-dyed fabrics, machine-pieced, hand-appliquéd **0392** Hand-dyed fabric pieced in bargello pattern, embellished with ink drawing, stitched,

quilted **0393** *Doodles*, 8" x 8" (20.3 x 20.3 cm), cotton, fused appliquéd, machine-quilted **0394** *Moths in Flight*, 12" x 24" (30.5 x 61 cm), cottons, synthetic lace, cotton wadding, Tyvek ink-jet printed, commercially produced stamp, Stazon stamping ink, Inktense pencils, Procion MX dyes, machine-piecing, machine-quilting, Tyvek digitally-printed **0395** Rusty Saw Blade. **0396** Abstract **0397** *Desire Lines #5*, hand-dyed cotton, free-form–pieced, machine-quilted **0398** *Orca*, 7" x 10" (17.8 x 25.4 cm), yarn, touring with the SAQA 25th Anniversary Exhibit **0399** *Lanikai* (detail) **0400** *One Mossy Stone* (detail) **0401** *Passages*, Two (detail) **0402** *Kona Sunset*, 45" x 36" (114.3 x 91.4 cm) hand-dyed cotton, silk; machine appliquéd, free-motion quilted **0403** *Potato Blues*, 12" x 8" (30.5 x 20.3 cm), free machine-quilted **0404** *The Green and Purple Balcony*, 8.25" x 13.12" (21 x 33.3 cm), digitally printed and hand-dyed cotton, pearl cotton, silk/bamboo batting. Hand-embroidered **0405** *Remix Africa*, 39" x 23" (99 x 59 cm), hand-dyed and commercial cottons, barkcloth, silks, pom-poms, machine-pieced, appliquéd, embroidered, quilted **0406** *Bat in the Moon*, 22" x 22" (56 x 56 cm), bleach discharged, rust-printed, hand-dyed fabric **0407** *Crossroads* (corner), velvets, silks, satins, embellished **0408** *Crossroads* (close up), décor trims, beads, ribbons, fabrics **0409** Contemporary mixed techniques **0410** *Intersections* **0411** Contemporary pieced **0412** *Cultivated Landscape* series **0413** Abstract **0414** Embellished crazy quilt detail **0415** *Petunias* (small quilt), raw-edge appliquéd, commercial batik cotton, free-motion quilted **0416** Shears I, 8" x 10" (20.3 x 25.4 cm) **0417** Contem-porary mixed techniques **0418** Constructed entirely of scraps, using only tones of light and dark **0419** *Crazy Quilt* **0420** *Between #2*, 10" x 15" (25.4 x 38 cm), silk and cotton fabric, thread, organza ribbon, recycled fabrics, machine-stitched **0421** *You Are Here*, 20" x 20" (51 x 51 cm), hand-dyed and commercial cotton fabrics, organza, silk organza ribbon, pompoms, machine-stitched, fused fabrics **0422** *Barrier and Moonrise*, each 12" (30.5 cm)

Chapter 3

0423 Gallery-wrapped canvas, 12" x 12" (30.5 x 30.5 cm), hand-painted fabrics and papers, cotton fabrics, acrylic paint and mediums, polyester batting, machine-quilted **0424** *Jellyfish*, hand-dyed fabric, silk, rayon thread, satin and organza ribbons, machine-appliquéd, embroidered **0425** *Fish Story*; photo: Casey Rae/Red Elf **0426** *Cuttlefish*, 12" x 12" (30.5 x 30.5 cm), free-motion openwork embroidery, ink transfer, raw-edge appliquéd using silk and synthetic fabrics, machine-quilted **0427** *Paisleyfish*, 12" x 12" (30.5 x 30.5 cm), paint, fabric, thread, painted whole cloth, thread painting **0428** *Broken Ginkgos III*, 12" x 12" (30.5 x 30.5 cm) cotton fabric and thread, free-motion quilted **0429** *Broken Ginkgos V*, 12" x 12" (30.5 x 30.5 cm), cotton fabric and thread, free-motion quilted **0430** *Broken Ginkgos II*, 12" x 12" (30.5 x 30.5 cm), cotton fabric and thread, free-motion quilted **0431** Figurative **0432** Cotton, tulle, quilted **0433** Landscape **0434**

Nature **0435** Nature **0436** *Clairière 1*, cotton batiks, cotton commercial fabrics, cotton batting, rayon threads, thermo-fused appliqué, free-hand, machine-quilted **0437** *Clairière 3*, cotton batiks, cotton commercial fabrics, cotton batting, rayon threads, thermo-fused appliqué, sewn by machine and free-hand, machine-quilted **0438** *Clairière 4*, 8" x 8" (20 x 20 cm), cotton batiks, cotton commercial fabrics, cotton batting, rayon threads, thermo-fused appliqué, sewn by machine and free-hand machine-quilted **0439** *Clairière 6*, 8" x 8" (20 x 20 cm), cotton batiks, cotton commercial fabrics, cotton batting, rayon threads, thermo-fused appliqué, sewn by machine and free-hand machine-quilted **0440** Landscape **0441** Figurative **0442** Figurative **0443** Figurative **0444** Figurative **0445** *Rainy Day*, fused, appliquéd, machine-quilted **0446** *A Night on the Ice*, UltraChrome ink on cotton, digital printing **0447** Feast #2, UltraChrome ink on cotton, digital printing **0448** *Ding-a-Ling*, UltraChrome ink on cotton, digital printing **0449** Landscape **0450** *Coastal View*, 28" x 21" (72 x 55 cm), cotton, rayon, metalic net, Angelina Fibres, sequins, metalic threads, fabrics on confetti-styled shapes embellinshed onto a surface with water-soluble fabrics, appliquéd, stitched **0451** *Eye On You*, 9.25" x 7.12" (23.5 x 18 cm), digital image, cotton fabric, cotton floss, fiber-reactive, hand-dyed cotton, cotton batting, polyester thread, embroidered **0452** *Early Riser*, 11.5" x 8.5" (29.2 x 21.6 cm) cotton, tulle, chiffon, upholstery fabrics and satin, layered fabric, free-motion quilted **0453** *Bird Of Paradise*, 6.5" x 4.5" (16.5 x 11.4 cm), chiffon layered with pale blue cotton, stippled, raw-edge appliquéd, free-motion quilted **0454** Conceptual **0455** Gallery wrapped canvas, 12" x 12" (30.5 x 30.5 cm), cotton fabrics, watercolor, acrylic mediums, paper, polyester batting **0456** *Consider the Kelp*; photo: David R. Wright **0457** *Endangered Reef*, hand-dyed and painted cotton, silk, velvet, raw-edge appliquéd, machine-stitched **0458** In The Woods, 11.75" x 11.75" (29.8 x 29.8 cm), free-motion machine embroidered, hand-embroidered on painted cotton **0459** Trees of the Swamp, 11.5" x 11.5" (29 x 29 cm), free-motion machine embroidered, hand-embroidered on painted cotton **0460** *Late Fall*, 12" x 8" (30.5 x 20.3 cm) free-motion machine-embroidered, hand-embroidered on painted cotton **0461** *Light Through the Trees*, 12" x 9" (30.5 x 23 cm) free-motion machine-embroidered, hand-embroidered on painted cotton **0462** *Endless Rhythms* (detail), silk, hand-dyed cotton, cheesecloth, beads, embroidery, torn fabrics, embellished, hand-embroidered **0463** Changing Seasons,(detail), hand-dyed fabric, paper, beads, and metal shim, assemblage of cutout leaves, machine-stitched, couched cords, beads **0464** *Cranes Passing Through*, 15" x 15" (38 x 38 cm), photo montage, heat transfers on layered organza over cotton **0465** *Red Orchids*, 15" x 15" (38 x 38 cm), photo montage, heat transfers on cotton **0466** Nature **0467** Nature **0468** *Season of Growth* (detail) **0469** *Jack in the Pulpit*, monoprint on cotton, stitched **0470** *Calm Before the Storm*, (detail), suede, ribbons, and beads, free-motion quilted **0471** Photo: Volker Lampe **0472** Nature **0473** Nature **0474** *Big Leaf 29*

0475 *Morning Breeze*, cotton sateen, free-motion quilted **0476** *Dandelions and Dragonflies*, appliquéd, needle-felted **0477** *Leaves*, 16" x 16" (40.6 x 40.6 cm) cottons and blends, machine appliquéd, machine-quilted **0478** Hand-dyed cotton, batting, tulle, fabric markers, cheesecloth, string, Trapunto, appliquéd, couched, fabric manipulation **0479** Nature **0480** *Suspicion*, ink, watercolor, and stitched on cotton **0481** *The Dance*, 12" x 12" (30.5 x 30.5 cm), assorted cotton fabrics, machine quilted **0482** *Silent Vigilance*, 8" x 8" (20.3 x 20.3 cm), cotton fabric, rayon thread, hand-appliquéd, embroidered, thread painting, confetti scraps, and machine-quilted **0483** *Esperanza Hope for the Tamarins* **0484** *Sitting Pretty*, pieced and thread painted **0485** Photo: Peter Gardner **0486** *Moth Fairy* (detail), cotton and tulle **0487** *Mother Earth* **0488** *Portrait of Amelia Earhart One*, (1 of 3), makes up a triptyck titled Searching for Amelia **0489** *Series Gestures: What Do You Fear?* (4 panels, each 19" x 14" (48.3 x 35.6 cm) **0490** *What Do You Fear?*, (4 panels, each 19" x 14" [48.3 x 35.6 cm]), cotton, net, latex, synthetic leather, painted whole cloth with applications, machine-quilted, embroidered, **0491** Cotton fabric and threads, appliquéd, and free-motion quilted **0492** *First Time*, 12" x 12" (30.5 x 30.5 cm) **0493** Peaceful, fabric and thread on canvas **0494** *Bayeux*, 10" x 10" (25.4 x 25.4 cm), linen, hick machine threads, free machine stitching **0495** *Balance* 2, 12" x 12" (30.5 x 30.5 cm) screen-printed, stenciled, machine-quilted **0496** *Rush* (four pieces), fabric and thread stretched onto wooden supports **0497** *Out in the Cold*, fabric and thread on canvas **0498** *In Her Footsteps*, fabric and thread on canvas **0499** Hand-painted, airbrushed, hand-quilted **0500** *The Wonder of Nature*, 20" x 20" (50.8 x 50.8 cm), cotton fabric, cotton batt, cotton thread, acrylic paint, airbrushed with acrylics, hand-painted and quilted, Photo: Robert Comings **0501** *Tesoro Escondido* **0502** *Speed*, 12" x 8" (30.5 x 20.3 cm), cotton fabric, thread, textile paint, screen printing, stenciling, machine quilting, Photo: Larry Stein **0503** *Tagged* **0504** *Work Day Dusk* **0505** Photo: Larry Goldstein Photograph **0506** *Uncanned Heat*, fabric and found-object collage. **0507** *View from the Academy*, 11" x 8.5" (28 x 21.6 cm), hand-dyed cotton, heavy-weight cotton thread, fused, machine-stitched **0508** *Berkhamsted #3*, 6" x 8" (15.2 x 20.3 cm). hand-dyed cotton, heavy-weight cotton thread, fused and machine-stitched **0509** *Two Pears*, fabric collaged, glued, fused **0510** *Good Morning*, fusible web, white tulle, pieced and stitched **0511** *Border Collie*, appliquéd, quilted **0512** *Baby*, photo print on fabric, fused, thread painted, needle-punched cat fur **0513** Quilted giclee on cotton **0514** *South Downs*, 10" x 10" (25.4 x 25.4 cm) calico, paint, newsprint, appliquéd, machine-stitched **0515** *Spring Shower*, fused, free-motion quilted **0516** Nature **0517** Photo: Gregory Case **0518** *Desert Blooms* **0519** Indian Paintbrush **0520** *Foundling Snow*, PanPastel and alcohol inks, dyed and stitched **0521** *Mysterious Turquoise Woods*, commercial fabric with appliquéd trees **0522** *Raise Your Hand*, machine and hand-stitched **0523** Cotton fabrics, machine-quilted and thread-painted **0524** Commercial cotton fabrics and acrylic inks, fusible appliquéd and machine-quilted **0525** *Gingko Trio*, (1 of 8-piece series), batik fabrics and couched cording stems **0526** Ginko Seasonal Trio, 22" X 23" (56 x 58.4 cm), cotton fabrics, batting, thread, hand-appliquéd, couched, machine-sewed, sashiko stitched **0527** Fruit Still Life on Black and White **0528 0529** Nature **0530** *San Francisco Square*, Santa Fe, 12" x 12" (30.5 x 30.5 cm), hand-dyed cotton and organza, raw-edge appliquéd, machine-quilted, hand-embroidered **0531** *Hollyhocks at the Museum of Art*, Santa Fe, 12" x 12" (30.5 x 30.5 cm), hand-dyed cotton, raw-edge appliquéd, machine-quilted, hand-embroidered **0532** *Looking Back*, 12" x 12" (30.5 x 30.5 cm) **0533** Landscape **0534** Nature **0535** Quilt showing texture achieved by fabric manipulation techniques; photo: Tom VanEynde **0536** Quilt showing texture achieved by fabric manipulation techniques, photo: Tom Van Eynde **0537** Nature **0538** *Oh, the Blues!*, floral fabrics **0539** *Poppy Fields*, free-motion quilted, strip-pieced and decorative machine-stitched, free-motion stitched **0540** *Art Poppies II*, pieced squares, decorative stitched, thread painted, hand-beaded embellishments **0541** *Bird of Paradise* (journal quilt) **0542** Nature **0543** Interesting Color for a Blackbird **0544** *Zebra Longwing Life Cycle* **0545** *Wings of Fire* **0546** *Emerged* **0547** *Red Rooster*, 13.5" x 13.5" (34.3 x 34.3 cm) raw-edge appliquéd, embroidered **0548** *Hello, Sunshine*; Photo: David R. Wright **0549** *Figurative* **0550** *Ephemeral Hues*, (detail), cotton batik and cotton print fabric, original design, machine-pieced, fused, machine-appliquéd, free-motion, machine-quilted **0551** *Ephemeral Hues*, (detail), cotton batik and cotton print fabric, original design, machine-pieced, fused, machine-appliquéd, free-motion, machine-quilted **0552** Commercial fabrics. Reverse appliquéd and bound **0553** *Singularity*, cotton, polyester thread, free-motion quilted **0554** *Mind-Manifesting Mask III*, cotton, polyester thread, free-motion quilted **0555** *Corinthian*, 12" x 12" (30.5 x 30.5 cm), photo manipulated in Photoshop, printed on silk organza, stitched and machine-quilted **0556** *Kaleidoscope Sky* **0557** Landscape **0558** Nature **0559** Photo: Ketterling Photography, Aberdeen, SD **0560** Landscape **0561** *Nature's Palette* **0562** *Lavender Fields of Provence* **0563** *Coastline*, 8" x 10" (20.3 x 25.4 cm) **0564** *Sea Stack at Sunset*, 18" x 20" (45.7 X 50.8 cm), cotton fabrics and batiks, Angelina Sheets, distressed acrylic felt, paint sticks, embroidery threads, black ink, paint, raw-edge appliquéd, thread embroidered, hand-painted, quilted **0565** Nature **0566** *Holy Land Landscape Sea of Galilee*, quilt art wall hanging, 15" x 19" (38 x 48.3 cm), cotton fabric, cotton batting, machine-pieced, appliquéd, quilted **0567** *Grandmother's Vineyard*, assorted hand-dyed, hand-woven silks, free-motion embroidered **0568** *Boreal Forest* **0569** All designs and creations by the artist. Most photos by the artist; others by Bruce McMillan **0570** Painted tea bags fused and quilted to fabric base and embellished with beads and charms **0571** *With Love from Holland*, appliquéd **0572** *Approaching Autumn*, 7" x 5" (17.8 x 12.7 cm), black cotton, hand-dyed cotton, crayons, embroidery thread, lined with Steam-a-Seam. **0573** *Almost Finished*, 8" x 6" (20.3 x 15 cm), hand-dyed cotton, Steam-a-Seam, black cotton, Shiva Sticks, embroidery thread, hand-embroidered **0574** *Bloom* **0575** *Dogwood in Autumn Wind I*, cotton, hand-dyed and painted fabric, raw-edge appliquéd, machine-quilted, hand-embroidered **0576** Hand-dyed, hand-painted fabrics, papers, felt batting, acrylic paint **0577** *Seedpods and Leaves*, 9.25" x 9.25" (25 x 25 cm) fused fabric, handmade paper, barkcloth background, pompoms, machine-stitched, fused **0578** Nautilus **0579** *Floral Landscape*, floral fabrics, fussy-cut, appliquéd **0580** Contemporary mixed techniques **0581** Contemporary mixed techniques **0582** Original design **0583** *Millennium Portal No. 3*, 72" (183 cm), machine-stitched and embroidered, repurposed paintings **0584** *Blue Leaves*, White Trees, 16.5" x 18" (42 x 45.7 cm), archival pigment inks printed on silk charmeuse and silk noil, digital art created from photos printed, layered, fused, appliquéd, free-motion, machine-quilted **0585** *Highlands Fall* (detail), hand-dyed, machine-pieced, machine-quilted **0586** *Cell Structure #8*, 6.5 x 6.5 (16.5 x 16.5 cm) wool and viscose felt, cotton backing, polyester thread, reverse-appliquéd, machine-stitched **0587** *The Ocean's Currency*, discharged fabrics, commercial fabrics, hand-dyed silk, free-motion embroidered and embellished **0588** *Nest*, Cyanotype over batik on cotton **0589** *Three Gentoos*, 2" x 12" (30.5 x 30.5 cm), jacquard silk, oilstiks, acrylics, painted, free-motion stitched **0590** *The White Hat*, 10" x 7" (25.4 x 17.8 cm), cotton batik, solid, mesh, and print; polyester sheer, brocade, and knit; rayon embroidery thread, prismatic foil, colored pencils, fusible fleece, beads, appliquéd, fused, machine-embroidered, quilted, beaded **0591** Courtesy: Blue Door Gallery, Yonkers, NY **0592** *Flag for the Americans*, machine-stitched **0593** Sweet Potatoes Don't Grow On Trees, full view and detail quilted, weaved, felted, beaded **0594** *Fencepost*, 10" x 8" (25.4 x 20.3 cm), wool roving, cotton and silk fabrics, pieced, machine felted, quilted **0595** *Of the Earth VIII*, 10" x 10" (25.4 x 25.4 cm) commercial cotton, batiks, linen, willow branches, innovative piecing, machine-quilted **0596** Snow-dyed fabric, printed photo on fabric **0597** *The End of Beauty*, Tyvek, scored organza, chiffon, angelina fibers, textiva film, sheer organza, free-machine stitched, painted, and free-motion stitched **0598** *Rising Sun*; photo: Nancy Dobson **0599** *A Forest Surprise*, (detail), cotton velveteen fabric, embroidery floss, perle cotton, crochet cotton, paper-cloth, acrylic paint, layering of hand-embroidered stitching, free-motion machine stitched, paper-cloth fabrication, crocheted **0600** *Riverbend* **0601** *Janusirsasana*, 28" x 46" (71 x 117 cm) **0602** *Ginkgos*, 12" x 12" (30.5 x 30.5 cm) **0603** *Ginkgos*, 12" x 12" (30.5 x 30.5 cm) **0604** Nature **0605** Nature **0606** Original design **0607** Transferred sketch to hand-dyed fabric, quilted and embellished and hand embroidered **0608** *The Beachhouse*, fused, appliquéd, photo-printed on fabric **0609** Raw-edge appliquéd, hand-embroidered **0610** *Coming Home I* **0611** *City Marina* **0612** *Tango Street*, 22" x 25" (60 x 63.5 cm), commercial and hand-dyed cotton fabrics, cotton batting, cotton and rayon thread strip piecing, reverse appliquéd, machine-quilted **0613** *A Garden Enclosed is My Sister, My Spouse*, 10" x 7" (25 x 18 cm) hand-dyed silk, commercial silk, screen printed, collaged, fused, machine-quilted **0614** *The Colourful Turban*, 6" x 8" (15.2 x 20.3 cm), calico, cotton fabric, paint, appliquéd, and machine-stitched **0615** Moon Dance, appliquéd **0616** *Summer in Virginia*, vintage feed sack, batik fabrics, ultra suede, hand-dyed felted wool, hand-embroidered and beaded, machine-quilted **0617** *Nemesis* (companion piece), bobbin work, machine appliquéd, stamped images and couching **0618** Photo: J. Haddrick **0619** *Cry Me a River*, 53" x 17" (134 x 43 cm), machine-appliquéd, diamond-pieced techniques **0620** *Rose Garden*, 12" x 12" (30.5 x 30.5 cm) **0621** *SABA Sunset*, 9" x 13" (23 x 33 cm), hand-dyed and commercial printed cotton, texture magic, dyed, pieced, free-motion quilted **0622** Landscape **0623** *Stuckagain Sunset*, 14.25" x 43" (35.7 x 109 cm), hand-dyed and commercial cottons, thread, water-soluble stabilizer, acrylic paint, squares placed on batting and backing, stitched in place using water-soluble stabilizer, thread embellishment highlighted **0624** *Ripening*, cotton, silk organza and other silk fabrics, raw-edge collaged, and machine-stitched **0625** Appliquéd 17" x 17" (43.2 x 43.2 cm) **0626** *Tangy Glen Bluebells*, commercial fabric, hand-dyed cheesecloth, hand-painted Tyvek and cords **0627** Commercial and hand-dyed cotton, fused, machine-quilted, hand-embroidered **0628** *The Moon Above Sees it All* (detail), cloth weaving, raw-edge appliquéd, hand-turned, couched, embroidered, hand-dyed nontraditional fabrics including linen, silk, and vintage textiles. **0629** *Chokecherries*, strip-pieced, hand-dyed and painted, free-form cut, raw-edge appliquéd, machine-embroidered, machine-quilted **0630** *Color in the Woods*, free-motion, machine-embroidered on dyed and painted fabrics **0631** *Summer Color*, free-motion, machine-embroidered on dyed fabric **0632** *Only the Ghosts of Leaves*, 26" x 16" (66 x 66 cm), hand-dyed and commercial cotton fabrics, silk, soluble fabric, machine appliquéd, trapunto and quilting, thread painting fabric painted, stitched text in borders **0633** Figurative **0634** Nature **0635** *Karen's Rose*, 6" x 6" (15 x 15 cm), commercial cottons **0636** *Poppies*, 12" x 12" (30.5 x 30.5 cm), hand-dyed and commercial cotton fabric, machine-pieced,raw-edge appliquéd, machine-quilted **0637** Hand-painted fabric and thread painted **0638** *Waiting for Spring*, quilted tone-on-tone cotton fabrics **0639** *Center of Attention* **0640** Appliquéd and hand-painted **0641** *Experience Texas* **0642** *The Painted Desert* (1st in the Earth in Three Bands: R, G, B series), hand-painted, thread painted, stitched, free-motion quilted **0643** *Snow Slices* **0644** *Munching Lunch*, 12" x 12" (30.5 x 30.5 cm), raw-edge appliquéd, embellished with yarn, machine-quilted **0645** Hand-dyed cotton and cheesecloth, machine-quilted, hand-couched, metallic yarn **0646** *Bunny II*, 14" x 13" (35.6 x 33 cm) thread-painted **0647** *Do Not Feed*, raw-edge appliquéd, couched **0648** *Landscape with Yellow Birds*, hand-appliquéd using batik fabrics, hand-quilted **0649** *My Weimaraner, Charlie*, designed from a photograph **0650** *Dragonfly* **0651** Linen **0652** *Arabesque Brown: Postcards from Jerusalem* **0653** Figurative **0654** *South Window*, 12.75" x 9.75" (32 x 25 cm), canvas, cotton, acrylic paint, free-motion thread painted on canvas, machine-quilted **0655** *The Life of Flowers*, wool, hand-dyed and commercial-dyed fabrics, hand-appliquéd, hand-pieced, hand-quilted **0656** *Thinking About a Crow*, 12" x 12" (30.5 x 30.5 cm) cotton, stitched, painted, and patchworked **0657** *Stained Glass Holy Land Landscape Sailboat*, fiber-art wall hanging, 15.75" x 22.25" (40 x 56.5 cm) cotton fabric, cotton batting, black tulle, appliquéd, machine-quilted **0658** *Rainy Day People*, fused, raw-edge appliquéd **0659** *Midwest Monsoonn*, 8" x 10" (20.3 x 25.4 cm) **0660** *The Rose I*, 11.25" x 9" (28 x 23 cm), raw-edge appliquéd, thread-painted, free-motion quilted **0661** *Moneyplant*, Thermofax screen print from original photo on hand-dyed cotton, machine-quilted, embellished, hand-stitched and vintage lace **0662** *In Five Directions* **0663** *Gold Bananas*, cotton and silk fabrics, watercolor pencils, oil pastels, raw-edge collaged, glued **0664** Machine-pieced, fused, raw-edge appliquéd, machine-quilted **0665** *Funky Trees*, hand-dyed fabrics, fused, raw-edge appliquéd, free-motion quilted **0666** *A Tree in a Landscape*, 6" x 6" (15 x 15 cm) appliquéd with tulle and embroidery appliquéd **0667** *Scenes from the Holy Land: The Windy Path*, fiber-art wall hanging, 17.5" x 19.5" (44.5 x 49.5 cm), cotton fabric, cotton batting, tulle, wool fibers, appliquéd, machine-quilted layer of tulle **0668** *Planting Seeds*, 18" x 18" (45.7 x 45.7 cm), commercial cottons and hand-dyed fabrics, reverse-appliquéd, hand-embellished, machine-pieced and quilted **0669** Photo: Petronella Ytsma **0670** *Fall in the Okanagan*, 5" x 8" (12.7 x 20.3 cm) hand-painted fabric, pieced, thread-painted, and hand-appliquéd **0671** *Anemone I*, 28" x 46" (71 x 117 cm) **0672** *Britt and Me*, raw-edge appliquéd, thread-painted details **0673** *Fire at Night*, commercial synthetic fabrics and beads, machine-stitched **0674** *Afternoon*, commercial cotton fabrics, machine-pieced, hand-appliquéd, hand-quilted **0675** *Tower of David* **0676** *She Sits to Create* (1 of 12) 6" x 6" (15 x 15 cm) hand-embroidered **0677** *Sahalie*, photographs abstracted and textured with Photoshop, digitally printed **0678** *The Painted Hills* (detail of an 89" [228 cm] panorama), hand-dyed cottons, linens, denim, and canvas, raw-edge appliquéd **0679** *Yum Yum Bay*, 8.5" x 11" (21.6 x 28 cm), cotton fabric, tulle, organza, rayon, cotton and silk threads, hand-appliquéd, hand and machine thread embroidered, painted highligjhts, machine-quilted

Chapter 4

0680 *Counter Culture '60s Style*, cotton, ric rac, button, embroidery floss, ribbon, handmade, hand-quilted, crochet **0681** *Art Is Healing*, 12" x 12" (30.5 x 30.5 cm), fabric, beads, shells, acrylic paint, machine-pieced, machine-quilted, hand-embellished and painted **0682** *Act As If*, 12" x 12" (30.5 x 30.5 cm), fabric, beads, shells, acrylic paint, machine-pieced, machine-quilted, hand-embellished and painted **0683** *First Things First*, 12" x 12" (30.5 x 30.5 cm), fabric, beads, shells, acrylic paint, machine-pieced, machine-quilted, hand-embellished and painted **0684** *Begin Now*, 12" x 12" (30.5 x 30.5 cm), fabric, beads, shells, acrylic paint, machine-pieced, machine-quilted, hand-embellished and painted **0685** Cotton satin, cotton duck, silk organza, anipulated image with overprinting, hand-painted and stitched borders **0686** *Our Bodies*, 12" x 12" (30.5 x 30.5 cm), digital media, natural textiles, hand-tied with bookbinding method, painted, creatively stitched **0687** *The Last Leaf*, 12" x 12" (30.5 x 30.5 cm), natural textiles, digital media, creatively stitched and hand-tied with bookbinding method, painted **0688** *Shift Your Thinking*, watercolor and Inktense on muslin **0689** *When I Think of You*, 12" x 12" (30.5 x 30.5 cm), hand-dyed organza, printed, stenciled, painted, cyanotype sprayed, stitched **0690** *Cedar and Stone*, 12" x 12" (30.5 x 30.5 cm) **0691** *Windows* (detail), 12" x 12" (30.5 x 30.5 cm), cotton broadcloth, dye, textile paints, polyester, rayon, and polyester thread, embroidery thread, deconstructed screen print, painted, embellished, free-motion quilted, Photo: Bob Turan **0692** *Intersections #1*, 12" x 12" (30.5 x 30.5 cm), screen-printed, painted, stenciled, free-motion quilted, Photo: Bob Turan **0693** *Intersections #3*, 12" x 12" (30.5 x 30.5 cm), cotton broadcloth, dye, textile paints, rayon, and polyester thread, screen-printed, stenciled, painted, machine-quilted, embellished, Photo: Bob Turan **0694** 6.5" x 6.5" (16.5 x 16.5 cm), Wool and viscose felt, cotton backing, polyester thread, reverse appliquéd, machine stitched **0695** 7.5" x 7.5" (19 x 19 cm), Wool and viscose felt, cotton backing, polyester thread, reverse appliquéd, machine stitched **0696** *St. Jacob's Coleus*, hand-painted Reemay, hand-dyed cotton lawn, heavy machine-quilted, hand-painted **0697** *Floral Burst*, Reemay mask, hand-dyed silk dupioni, machine-quilted, hand-beaded **0698** *Lorikeet Circus*, hand-dyed cotton, free-form cut, pieced, machine-quilted **0699** *Flying Colors: King Parrot*, 12" x 12" (30.5 x 30.5 cm) free-form, pierced, machine-quilted **0700** *Tuning Fork #14*, 10" x 7" (25.4 x 17.8 cm), cotton fabrics, (commercial and hand-dyed),cotton thread, cotton/poly batting, machine-pieced, machine quilted **0701** *Ruins #3*, 12" x 12" (30.5 x 30.5 cm), cotton fabrics, (commercial and hand-dyed), cotton thread, cotton/poly batting, machine-pieced, machine quilted **0702** Photo: Julie R. Filatoff **0703** *A Sense of Place* (detail), hand-dyed, hand-printed cotton, machine-pieced and quilted **0704** *Ruins #4*, 61" x 42" (155 x 106 cm), cotton fabric, commercial and hand-dyed, cotton thread, cotton/poly batting, machine-pieced, machine-quilted **0705** *Ruins #1*, 83" x 65" (211 x 165 cm), cotton fabric, commercial and hand-dyed, cotton thread, cotton/poly batting, machine-pieced, machine-quilted **0706** Tulle, ink, yarns, paper, metal brads, couched fiber, hand and machine-stitched, appliquéd **0707** *Visible*, commercial fabrics, poly batting, hand-dyed, appliquéd, quilted **0708** Gallery wrapped canvas, 12" x 12" (30.5 x 30.5 cm) cotton fabrics, acrylic paint and mediums, inks, paper, polyester batting **0709** *Only Look at Me*, 10" x 13" (25.4 x 33 cm) cotton, recycled beer cans, PVC capsules, acrylic paint, collaged, machine-quilted **0710** *QR Code*, 8" x 8" (20.3 x 20.3 cm), woven, fused, machine-quilted **0711** *Physio-*

therapy, digital print, machine-quilted, Mod-podge paper detail, stenciled lettering **0712** Photo: Eric Neilsen, collection of Elisabeth de la Croix **0713** Photo: Eric Neilsen, collection of Linda Fowler **0714** Photo: Eric Neilsen, collection of Sandra Sider **0715** Photo: Eric Neilsen, collection of Beth Johnson **0716** Turquoise Table Runner, 15" x 40" (38 x 102 cm), cotton fabrics, machine-pieced, machine-quilted **0717** *Goldfinch Feeders*, 12" x 12" (30.5 x 30.5 cm) **0718** *Rain*, hand-dyed silk, cotton fabrics, folded, pleated, machine-quilted, raw-edge appliquéd, free-motion stitched **0719** *Think the Grass is Greener?*, fusible collage, hand-dyed fabrics, machine-appliquéd, quilted **0720** *Joint Effort (Kate)*, cyanotype photographs printed on cotton. Collection of Rocky Mountain Quilt Museum **0721** *Joint Effort (Charlie)*, machine-pieced cyanotype photographs on cotton. Collection of the Rocky Mountain Quilt Museum **0722** *Jewels*, machine-pieced, cyanotype photographs on fabric. Collection of the Rocky Mountain Quilt Museum **0723** *Log Loading Stanley*, Cyanotype photographs on cotton, machine embroidered, appliquéd, quilted **0724** *Tree Four*, machine-pieced, cyanotype photographs on cotton **0725** *Sengakuji*, machine-pieced cyanotype photographs, cotton fabric, machine-quilted **0726** *Kas Sawing Kerf*, machine-pieced cyanotype photographs and photograms on cotton, machine and reverse-appliquéd, double-needle stitched, machine-quilted **0727** *Coffee Dreamin'*, 10" x 8" (25.4 x 20.3 cm) manipulated/edited photo in Picasa, printed on fabric, machine-pieced and quilted **0728** *Little Latte*, Tsukineko inks, free-motion stitched **0729** *Inspire Airstream Dreaming Patchwork Urban Footscape* **0730** *Fire Fish Made*, 12" x 12" (30.5 x 30.5 cm), cotton, silk fabric and threads, free-motion quilted **0731** *I Heart Texture*, glass beads, couched fibers, Mono and screen-printed, ground pieced, stitched, appliquéd **0732** *Nature* **0733** iPad cover **0734** *Bead Creative*, handmade beads **0735** *The Ancient Beginning of a New World*, hand painted silk habotai, cotton, commercial color, velvet, direct appliquéd, machine-embroidered with silk thread, anilin dye with gutta resist **0736** *Henry's Haircut*, alpaca hair, machine-embellished, machine and hand-stitched, beaded **0737** *Digitally Altered*, hand-stitched **0738** Pearl, 6" x 6" (15.2 x 15.2 cm) **0739** *Neapolitan*, fractal design, printed silk, hand-embroidered **0740** Abstract **0741** *Essence of Dobbins Lookout*, pieced and hand-appliquéd **0742** Abstract **0743** *Note for a Friend #1*, cotton fabric, raw-edge collaged, hand-embroidered, machine-stitched **0744** *Boundary Waters 5*, white cotton, felt, hand-dyed cheesecloth, hand-dyed cotton yarn and fabric, upholstery, polyester, silk fabrics, duck cloth, vintage polyester scarves, silk paper, velvet, netting. Painted, screen-printed, stamped, burned, crocheted, **0745** *Red Bioluminescence* **0746** *Three Sheets to the Wind* **0747** *Noonship* **0748** *Kantha*, hand-stitched on batik **0749** *Monster Mountain*, velvet, cottons, and embroidery floss **0750** *Sunlight on Water*, hand-dyed cottons, freezer paper, free-motion quilted to incorporate metallic and opalescent threads **0751** *Les Raisins (Grapes)*, hand-dyed Kona cottons, screened with metallic paints, free-motion quilted **0752** *Valley of Fire*, hand-dyed Kona cotton, silk, organza, raw-edge appliquéd, free-motion quilted **0753** Photo: Ron Weiss **0754** *Detail of Scape*, dyed and screen-printed silk and cotton, appliquéd, and pleated, free-motion machine-embroidered **0755** *Detail of Patina*, appliquéd with silk chiffon, machine- and hand-embroidered, quilted with free motion embroidery **0756** *Detail of Vestige*, printed cotton, free-motion embroidered, trappunto-quilted **0757** Abstract **0758** *Fragments #4*, 12″ × 12″ × 0.75″ (30.5 × 30.5 × 2 cm), vintage linens, cottons, dye-painted, screen-printed, machine-pieced, free-motion stitched **0759** *Currents #14*, 12″ × 12″ (30.5 × 30.5 cm), cottons, dye-painted, screen-printed, machine-pieced, appliquéd, free-motion stitched **0760** *Altered State*, original dotted upholstery fabric transformed with printing techniques, trapunto, and embellished **0761** Discharge dyed and over-dyed using ice dyeing, machine-pieced and machine-quilted **0762** *Faded Fragments* **0763** *Felt Fantasy 01*, synthetic felt, cotton threads, stitched, hand-beaded **0764** *Forest For The Trees* (detail), commercial print fabrics, porcupine quills, stone and glass beads, machine-quilted **0765** Abstract **0766** *Anping Tree House*, 12″ × 12″ (30.5 × 30.5 cm), cotton, lamé, oilstiks, acrylics, threads, painted, appliquéd, free-motion stitched **0767** *Counter Culture '60s Style*, recycled clothing, cotton, ric rac, jewelry fragments, embroidery floss, ribbon, handmade Grateful Dead patch, hand-sewn, hand-quilted, crocheted **0768** *Outlaw Skunk and Outlaw Rabbit* **0769** *Green Mansions*, 12″ × 12″ (30.5 × 30.5 cm), manipulated commercial and hand-dyed fabrics, collaged, hand-quilted **0770** *Asian Inspiration Series* **0771** *Fly Away*, design, creation, and photo by Ann Grundler **0772** *Straight Up*, design, creation, and photo by Ann Grundler **0773** *Northern Lights*, 12″ × 12″ (30.5 × 30.5 cm) **0774** 12″ × 12″ (30.5 × 30.5 cm), pieced cotton, wool batting; Quilted with walking foot **0775** Abstract **0776** Thread-painted **0777** *Spring* **0778** *Solar Flare*, 14″ × 14″ (35.6 × 35.6 cm), acrylic painted silk, cotton, canvas, cotton batting, layered, collaged, machine-quilted **0779** *Garden View* (detail), acrylic painted silk, cotton, canvas, cotton batting, layered, collaged, machine-quilted, Photo: John Tuckey **0780** 100% cotton fabric textured with modeling paste, pumice gel, lava gel, and clear tar gel, painted and hand-stitched. **0781** 100% white cotton, batting and backing, machine-stitched with black thread, textured with modeling paste, painted with acrylic paint **0782** *Convergence*, (detail), hand-dyed fabric, bleach, rust, oil pastel, pastel pencil **0783** *Ammonite VIII*, 12″ × 12″ (30.5 × 30.5 cm) **0784** *Flutter V*, 10″ × 10″ (25.4 × 25.4 cm) **0785** *Time Flies*, 10″ × 10″ (25.4 × 25.4 cm) **0786** All original designs, hand-dyed cotton **0787** Silk, cotton, phototransfered, appliquéd **0788** *Boundary Waters* 28, screen-printed and painted, hand and machine-stitched **0789** Details of larger original hand-dyed cotton quilts **0790** *Currents #26*, 12″ × 12″ (30.5 × 30.5 cm), vintage linens, cottons, dye-painted, screen-printed, machine-pieced, appliquéd, free-motion stitched **0791** *Epic Journey Modello* **0792** *Eleven 3 Thirteen*, appliquéd transparent silks on

hand-dyed cotton with stamping, hand-stitched with pearled cotton **0793** *Eleven 3 Eleven*, dry-brush painted on hand-dyed cotton, appliquéd commercial cotton, transparent silks, hand-stitched with pearled cotton **0794** *Class of 1935*, hand-painted silk with resist, hand-stitched with pearled cotton, hand-appliquéd cord and transparent silks **0795** *Fudge Box*, hand-painted silk with resist, hand-appliquéd transparent silks, hand-stitched with pearled cotton **0796** *Dunes at the Beach*, hand-painted silk with resist, hand-stitched with pearled cotton, hand-appliquéd transparent silks **0797** *Daguerre*, Meet Mondrian, 12″ ×12″ (30.5 × 30.5 cm), hand-dyed, solar-printed, acrylic-painted cotton fabric, cotton thread, cotton batting, stenciled, dip-dyed, solar printed, straight-line quilted **0798** Series of canyon wall quilts, 14″ × 12″ (35.6 × 30.5 cm) framed, hand-dyed and commercial fabrics **0799** *Canyonlands 2 Dusk*, 16″ × 20″ (40.6 × 50.8 cm), hand-dyed material, batik, pieced and stitched with King Tut thread; photo: John Sims **0800** Reproduction; photo: Taylor Dabney **0801** Abstract **0802** Abstract **0803** *Zip City Zippers* **0804** *Sisters* **0805** *A Far Away Galaxy*, colorful fabrics from the floor of a tailor shop in New York who fashions African women's clothing **0806** *Three Wishes*, velour, taffeta, satin, tulle, felt, copper, metal zippers, machine and hand-stitched, row edge appliquéd **0807** *Sweet Life*, hand-dyed and commercial fabrics, candy wrappers, tulle, netting, found objects, heat-bonded appliqué, machine-stitched **0808** *Tide Pool*, machine-stitched fiber fragments, mixed content fibers, tulle overlays, heat-bonded appliqué **0809** *Inside Out*, hand-painted cotton batting, open, machine-stitched threadwork,using threads, cords, yarns, hand and machine-stitched **0810** *Immer nie genug (Ever never enough)*, (detail), cotton, acrylic paints, fiber-reactive dyes, cotton thread, hand-dyed, printed, silk screened, machine-stitched **0811** *Currents #22*, (detail), machine-pieced, appliquéd, free-motion stitched **0812** Landscape **0813** *Outspoken*, hand-dyed cotton, heat-bonded appliqué, machine-embroidered, machine-quilted **0814** *Arcade*, nontraditional fibers on a hand-dyed base. **0815** *Brentwood Barn* (detail), canvas, cotton, acrylic paint, free-motion thread painted, machine-quilted **0816** *Mending Fences* (detail), canvas, cotton, acrylic paint, free-motion thread painted on canvas, machine-quilted **0817** Designs and photos: Judith Mundwiler **0818** *Quail Cottage Barn*, 23″ × 24″ (58.4 × 61 cm), canvas, cotton, acrylic paint, free-motion thread painted, machine-quilted **0819** *Nerites* variations **0820** Agapanthus Sunset **0821** Cotton fabrics, machine-appliquéd, embellished, 4.75″ × 4.75″ (12 × 12 cm) **0822** Abstract **0823** *Twisted Hornet and Little Fantasy*, hand-dyed fabric, pieced, and free-motion quilted **0824** Abstract **0825** Abstract **0826** Abstract **0827** *Abstract Series*, hand-dyed fabric, machine doodling **0828** Abstract **0829** *Reflections*, cotton, silk fabrics, raw-edge collaged, hand- and machine-stitched **0830** Photo: Petr Nikodem **0831** *Titanium*, radical elements series, landscape fabric, wool fleece, grommets, heavy wool quilted with felt needles, hand-quilted **0832** *Cruciform #2*, cotton fabrics, water-soluble pastels, raw-edge collaged, painted **0833** Photo: Petr Nikodem **0834** Photo: Petr Nikodem **0835** Conceptual **0836** Conceptual **0838** Abstract **0839** *Zentangle in Reemay*, Reemay, commercially printed fabric, machine-quilted, beaded **0840** All original designs, hand-dyed cotton **0841** Folded, pleated, scrunched, stitched, painted **0842** *Hot*, Lumiere textile paints on black fabric, seed beads, quilted **0843** *Night Fall*, folded, pleated, scrunched, stitched, painted **0844** *One Life*, assorted fabrics and fibers, some hand-dyed, free-motion embroidered **0845** *New Beginnings*, Rust printed whole cloth, acrylic painted canvas, hand-stitched, inked colors, hand-beaded, embroidered **0846** Contemporary mixed techniques **0847** *Life Study #5*, painted, fused, free-motion quilted **0848** *Life Study #15*, painted, free-motion quilted **0849** Abstract **0850** *Different Perspectives I*, (detail), 100% cotton, fusible interfacing, black/white, and 11 different values of grey thread; free-motion thread painted **0851** 100% black Kona cotton discharged with chlorine bleach, antichlor, and viox, pieced and fused **0852** Conceptual **0853** *Fly Me To The Moon* **0854** *Canadian Sunrise* **0855** Discharged design, 12" x 12" (30.5 x 30.5 cm) pieced and machine-quilted **0856** *Checkpoint*, 54" x 57" (137 x 145 cm), Mylar fabric, painted canvas **0857** *Alternating Currents*, 48" x 48" (122 x 122 cm) Mylar, fabric, painted canvas, gold leather, digital prints **0858** *Y or Why or ?... Because*, tea/coffee-dyed linen, vintage embroidered transfer, micron pen, hand-stitched with silk thread **0859** *Forgotten Wings*, 12" x 12" (30.5 x 30.5 cm), multilayered fiber photographs. Images printed on treated natural textiles and other surfaces **0860** *Leaving Home*, 12" x 12" (30.5 x 30.5 cm), multilayered fiber photographs, treated natural textiles, creatively stitched **0861** *In Disguise*, 12" x 12" (30.5 x 30.5 cm), treated natural textiles, segments held together with hand-tied bookbinding method, creatively stitched **0862** *Improvisational Curved Log Cabin*, pieced cottons, unquilted **0863** *Big Leaf Impromptu 14* **0864** *Big Leaf Impromptu 12* **0865** Designs and photos: Judith Mundwiler **0866** Designs and photos: Judith Mundwiler **0867** *Oh! Rock-a-My Soul!* **0868** *Going in Circles* **0869** Abstract **0870** *Time Space Motion*, 12" (30.5 cm) fabric collage **0871** *Destination*, 12" x 12" (30.5 x 30.5 cm) **0872** *Four Seasons: Summer*, (detail) **0873** Abstract **0874** *The Big Apple* (detail), silk, satin, tulle, glass beads, hand-appliquéd, quilted **0875** *Teeth* **0876** Free-motion, hand-embroidered, felted, and painted **0877** Hand-dyed cottons, machine-quilted **0878** Hand-dyed cotton fabrics, raw-edge appliquéd **0879** *Breathing and Barking*, organza, barkcloth from Uganda, silk, hand-dyed cotton, cotton string, raffia, machine-stitched, fused fabrics **0880** *Once This River Ran Wide and Deep*, 12" x 12" (30.5 x 30.5 cm), commercial cotton fabric, hand-stitched **0881** *When This River Ran Wide and Deep*, 12" x 12" (30.5 x 30.5 cm), commercial cotton fabric, stenciled, free-hand drawn, hand-stitched **0882** *Autumn Improvisation III*, 4.75" x 4.75" (12 x 12 cm), cotton fabrics, machine-appliquéd, embellished **0883** *Il y a toujours des idées pour un peu de soleil*, (detail), cotton, fiber-eactive dyes, pearl yarn, lace, painted,

printed, silkscreened, pieced, appliquéd, embroidered **0884** *Cosmic Vibrations*, 14" x 11" (35.6 x 28 cm) matted, hand-dyed and African batiks; photo: John Sims **0885** Cotton, fabric paint, thread, mono-printed, free-motion quilted, stenciled, stamped **0886** Cotton, linen, fabric paint, metallic thread, gel-printed, stamped, stenciled **0887** Anchor Up (detail) **0888** Abstract **0889** *Above It All*, felted and quilted collage **0890** *Four Seasons*, appliqué of mixed media: pieced fabric, felted yarn, collaged fabric, paper, paint, polymer clay millefiori **0891** *Rejuvenation* (detail) **0892** Photo: Tom van Eynde **0893** *Afterglow I* **0894** *Running Wild* **0895** *Landing* **0896** *Circle Dance* **0897** *Life In Our Family* **0898** *Build It*, appliquéd, quilt writing **0899** *Pecan Pie*, quilted, woven, beaded **0900** *Spine*, 7.5" x 14.25" (19 x 36 cm), small quilt, Mylar, fabric, painted canvas **0901** 12" x 12" (30.5 x 30.5 cm) **0902** *Hawaiian Beauty* (crop) **0903** Fabric and wool, fabric-painted, hand- and machine-embroidered, machine-quilted, appliquéd **0904** *A Drop of Life*, 38" x 41" (97 x 105 cm), cotton, wool embroidery thread and paint, fabric manipulation, machine-embroidered, open edge sewing, machine-quilted, hand-painted, appliquéd, Photo: Wessel Viljoen **0905** *Watching the Rain* **0906** *Open Studio Tarot, Number 47, The Gossip*, 4" x 6" (10 x 15 cm), series of mixed media postcards, Photo transfer, oil pastel, hand-dyed fabric **0907** *Open Studio Tarot, Number 5, The Caged Bird*, 4" x 6" (10 x 15 cm), series of mixed media postcards, photo transfer, hand-dyed fabric, oil pastel, paper, plastic mesh **0908** *I Felt Purple* (detail), 9" x 9" (23 x 23 cm), wool, synthetic felt, hand-dyed cotton fabric, cotton batting, cotton thread, yarn, ribbon, trim, machine-felted, raw-edge appliquéd **0909** *Benches*, 14" x 14" (35.6 x 35.6 cm) over-dyed cotton, hand-dyed cotton batting and fabrics, cotton batik, print fabrics, bamboo-cotton blend batting, raw-edge appliquéd, machine-quilted **0910** *Improvisational Block*, 8" (20.3 cm) **0911** Photo: Bernard W. Brooks **0912** *Graffiti*, painted and stitched paper, quilt mounted on painted canvas **0913** *Flow*, 23" x 18.5" (58.4 x 47 cm) white cotton canvas, free-hand drawn with Paintstiks, hand-embellished with beads, yarn, and threads **0914** Couched yarns, commercial fabrics, paper clay, and Lutradur, machine-quilted, appliquéd **0915** *All That Glitters*, 12" x 12" (30.5 x 30.5 cm), hand-dyed cotton, yarn, hologram thread, beads, Textiva, machine-quilted, embellished, appliquéd **0916** *Solitary*, 12" x 12" (30.5 x 30.5 cm), appliquéd, couched yarns, free-form quilted **0917** *Running Feather*, 15" x 15" (38 x 38 cm), photo montage, heat transfers on cotton **0918** Abstract **0919** *Cogs* **0920** *He Knew That She Knew That I Know*, triple white custom-printed fabric, Poly-fit, cotton batting, beads, machine-quilted, trapunto-stuffed, beaded **0921** *He Knew That She Knew That I Know*, triple white from custom-printed fabric, Poly-Fit, cotton batting, beads, custom-printed, machine-quilted, trapunto-stuffed, beaded **0922** *Cell Memories*, merino fleece, industrial felt, silk gauze, hand-painted, discharged, wet-felted, machine-quilted **0923** Hand-batiked, 24" x 30" (61 x 76 cm) 100% cotton damask, dyed pearled cotton threads, free-form pieced, hand quilted **0924** *Fireworks over the Alamo*, thread-painted **0925** *Birds of A Feather*, 12" x 12" (30.5 x 30.5 cm), suspended beads, raw-edge appliquéd fabric shapes **0926** *Storm Series: Wind*, 12" x 12" (30.5 x 30.5 cm) African batik, silk, and silk ribbon, pieced background of batik and silks, quilted, beaded, hand-dyed fabric; photo: John Sims **0927** *After The Rain* (detail) **0928** *Phoenix* (detail), 8 x 12 (20.3 x 30.5 cm), hand-dyed cotton, whole cloth, free-motion quilted, drawing **0929** *Arabian Door II*, 6.5" x 9.5" (16.5 x 24 cm) hand-painted cotton, surface designed with paint and thermofax screens, machine-quilted and framed **0930** Discharged cotton fabric, tulle, textile paint, beads, stenciled, appliquéd, beaded **0931** *In a Monastery Garden*, 10" x 8" (25.4 x 20.3 cm) screen-printed, appliquéd, pieced, machine-quilted **0932** *Detail of Flux*, dyed and discharge-printed on silk and cotton, appliquéd, free-motion stitched **0933** *Once Upon A Time, There Were Three Goddesses*, dyed cloth, screen-printed, hand- and machine-stitched **0934** *Arabian Java*, 12" x 12" (30.5 x 30.5 cm), hand-painted cotton fabric, surface designed, quilted **0935** *Detail View from Reverberations: Yellowstone Waters*, archival pigment inks printed on silk charmeuse digital art created from photos printed, layered, fused, appliquéd, free-motion, machine-quilted **0936** *Abstract* **0937** *Georgian Bay Sunset*, printed, painted, manipulated cotton using Color Vie pigments, pieced, fused **0938** *Golden Rain* **0939** *Perception*, three sections of one quilt **0940** Design, creation, and photo by Ann Grundler **0941** *Trees Along a Creek* **0942** *Confluence: Cloud Pattern No. 1*, machine-stitched, rag paper, silkscreened vinyl, holographic and silver Mylar, Pellon, AC-64, and polymer matt medium **0943** Photo: James Dewrance **0944** *The Ever-Changing Sky Behind Blossoms of Silk Cotton Trees*, commercial cottons, machine-pieced, yo-yo hand-appliquéd, hand-quilted **0945** *Cityscape No. 3 1977*, 84" x 84" (213 x 213 cm), machine stitched and interlaced, 16 mm microfilm, laundry tag paper, Lurex, cotton edging, Velcro machine-stitched and interlaced **0946** *The Hand of Fatima*, 8" x 9" (20.3 x 23 cm), cotton surface, thermo fax screening, hand-painted, heavily quilted **0947** *David*, fabric art portrait of director/actor David Ellenstein **0948** *In Town* **0949** *Gone With The Wind*, weaved, shibori dyed squares, dry felting and quilted **0950** *Peace in the Forest*, hand-dyed industrial paper towels, appliquéd, machine-quilted **0951** *House Dreaming* (detail) hand-dyed, machine-pieced, machine and hand-quilted **0952** *Ground Zero No. 10 Target Babylon IV, 1989*, interlaced, machine-stitched, embroidered, pieced **0953** *Scrap City*, 39" x 31" (100 x 80 cm), cotton, acrylic paints, fiber-reactive dyes, digital photos, scraps, rayon thread, hand-dyed, appliquéd, embroidered, machine-quilted **0954** *Tree*, combines mixed techniques and fibers. **0955** *Sea World*, 4" x 8" (10 x 20.3 cm) organza, beads, hand-embroidered **0956** *Nature* **0957** This work hangs away from a wall so that the air and wind move each segment. **0958** *Nature* **0959** *Nature* **0960** *Skywalker*, 45" x 33" (114 x 84 cm) hand-dyed silk, cotton, polyester thread, free-motion quilted, machine-appliquéd **0961** *Colony*, hand-dyed silk, cotton, polyester thread, free-motion quilted, machine-appliquéd **0962** *Low Tide* (mini), 7.5 x 7.5 (19 x 19 cm) wool and viscose felt, polyester net, polyester thread, reverse-appliquéd, machine-stitched **0963** *Bella Petite*, 10" x 7" (25.4 x 17.8 cm), acrylic painted silk, cotton, canvas, cotton batting, layered, collaged, machine-quilted **0964** *Cityscape No. 7 1978*, 84" x 84" (213 x 213 cm), machine-stitched and interlaced, 35-mm microfilm, laundry tag paper, opalescent Mylar, Lurex, paint, fabric-backed, eyelets **0965** *Millennium Satellite*, 1988, machine-stitched **0966** *Chimney* (detail) hand-dyed, tea-dyed, screen-printed, appliquéd and pieced, machine-quilted **0967** *Knock on Wood*, 12" x 12" (30.5 x 30.5 cm) **0968** *Four Rooms with a View* (detail) hand-dyed, pieced, machine-quilted **0969** *The Idea Is Born* (detail), silk, damask, gauze, silk cocoon, yarn, pearls, machine-pieced, hand-appliquéd **0970** Painted, stitched silk and cotton

Chapter 5
0971 *Fanfare #2: Floating Lotus* **0972** *3 x 3 #1: Cactus (New York)* **0973** *Garden Grid #3* **0974** *On the Road: Curves Ahead* **0975** *Penumbra #8: Love Letters* **0976** *Tutti Frutti* (detail) **0977** *Garden Grid #5* (detail) **0978** *Garden Grid #5* **0979** *Tutti Frutti* (detail) **0980** *On the Road: Curves Ahead* (detail) **0981** *Going Home* **0982** *Water Wheels* **0983** *Garden Grid #2* (detail) **0984** *Garden Grid #3* (detail) **0985** *Penumbra #7: Twilight* **0986** *Penumbra #7: Twilight* (detail) **0987** *Bottoms Up!* **0988** *Penumbra #2: Silent Soldiers* **0989** *Penumbra #3: Rule of Silence* **0990** *Bottoms Up!* (detail) **0991** *Women at Work and Play #7* **0992** *Penumbra #4: Reliquary* **0993** *Penumbra #4: Reliquary* (detail) **0994** *On the Road: Slippery When Wet* **0995** *On the Road: Slippery When Wet* (detail) **0996** *On the Road: Road Rage* **0997** *On the Road: Road Rage* (detail) **0998** *Boogie-Down Kitchen* **0999** *Chapultepec Flash* **1000** *Knight Watch*

Quilt Artist Directory

Amie Starchuk
amiestarchuk.com
0929, 0934, 0946

Ann Baldwin May
annbaldwinmayartquilts.com
0466

Ann Grundler
0219, 0220, 0770-0774, 940

Ann Ribbens
mnartists.org/artistHome.do?rid=341986
0669

Anna Gajewska
0806, 0812, 0872, 0873

Anne Smyers
housetohome.pro/art-quilts
0538, 0579

Anne Solomon
0777, 0936

Annemiek Te Pas-Aalders
0037, 0038

Annie Helmericks-Louder
helmericks.com
0768, 0769

Arja Speelman
arja-art.blogspot.com
0523, 0570, 0622

Arle Sklar-Weinstein
FiberFoto.com
0464. 0465, 0591, 0917

Arturo Alonzo Sandoval
arturoart.com
0583, 0592, 0942, 0945, 952, 964, 965

B J Adams
BJAdamsArt.com
0306, 0307, 0309, 0311, 312, 0373,
0434, 0435

Barbara Chapman
brushesandcloth.blogspot.ca
0568, 0688

Barbara Littlefield Wendt
0016, 0207

Barbara Triscari
triscartsi.com
0130

Barbara W. Watler
barbarawatler.com
0745-0747, 0854

Becky Grover
0269

Belinda Hart
belindahart.com
0750-752

Bella Kaplan
bellakaplan.com
0613

Benedicte Caneill
benedictecaneill.com
0349

Berta Goldbager
judaicafabricart.com
0300

Bethany E. Garner
bethanygarner.blogspot.ca
0923

Bob Mosier
0850

Bobbe Shapiro Nolan
bobbeshapironolan.weebly.com
0332

Bodil Gardner
bodilgardner.dk
0485

Brenda Gael Smith
brendagaelsmith.com
0276, 0282-0284, 0335, 0337,
0338, 0397, 0698, 0699

Brigitte Kopp
brigitte-kopp-textilkunst.eu
0489, 0490, 0492, 0948

Brigitte Morgenroth
morgenroth-quilts.de
0056, 0071-0074, 0129

Britta Ankenbauer
britta-ankenbauer.de stoffart.blogspot.
com
0810, 0883, 0953

Camilla Brent Pearce
0858

Candice L. Phelan
FiberArtVision.com
0384-0386, 0608

Carol Anne Grotrian
carolannegrotrian.com
0140

Carol Dickson
0741

Carol Larson
live2dye.com
0758, 0759, 0790, 0811

Carol Marshall
facebook.com/yannidesigns?fref=ts
0556

Carol Seeley
fibreartnetwork.com
0482, 0679

Carole Ann Frocillo
0805, 0905

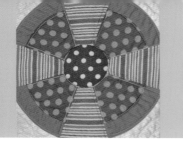

Caroline Sharkey
textileartworkshopsonline.com
0449, 0450

Carolyn Carson
carolyncarsonart.com
0753, 0757

Carolynn McMillan
rtquilter.blogspot.com
0569, 0626, 0696, 0697, 0763, 0839

Catherine Baltgalvis
0053, 0142

Cathy Spivey Mendola
cmendola.blogspot.com
0587

Chapultepec Flash
0999

Charity McAllister
humboldtcherry.blogspot.com
0680, 0767

Charlotte Ziebarth
0584, 0935

Cheryl Edwards
0359

Cheryl Olson
cherylolsonartquilts.com
0227, 0402, 0479, 0557–0560

Chris Dixon
0852

Christine Ravish
0368, 0611

Christine Seager
chrisse.co.uk
0270, 0271, 0272, 0855

Cindy Grisdela
cindygrisdela.com
0223, 0342

Cindy Richard
cindyrquilts.com
0075, 0314, 0350, 0566, 0657, 0667

Clairan Ferrono
fabric8tions.net
0765, 0892

Clara Nartey
ClaraNartey.com
0280, 0281

Coleen Adderley
coleenadderley.com
0637, 0670

Colleen Ansbaugh
ColleenAnsbaugh.com
0786, 789, 0840

Corinne Zambeek-van Hasselt
corinnezambeek.nl
0869

Cuauhtemoc Q. Kish
cuauhtemocqkishfabricartist.com
0947

Cynthia H. Catlin
0299, 0719, 0970

Dahlia Clark
dahliaclark.com
0847, 0848

Daniela Tiger
danielatiger.blogspot.ca
0418, 0607

Darleen N. Madsen
0026

David Charity
fromedge2edge.com
0706, 0914

Deanna Miller
0021

Deb Berkebile
0642

Deb Brockway
0550, 0551

Deborah Boschert
DeborahsStudio.com
0676, 0690

Deborah Lyn Stanley
lynstanleyart.com
0524

Denise Oyama Miller
deniseoyamamiller.com
0224, 0423, 0455, 0576, 0708

Diane Becka
dianebecka.com
0079, 0137–0139, 0393, 0710

Diane Duncan
0599

Diane Eastham
dianeeastham.com
0780, 0781, 0851

Diane Melms
dianemelms.com
0263–0266

Diane Wright
dianewrightquilts.blogspot.com
0456, 0548

Dianne Browning
bendartquilts.com
0407, 0408, 0470, 0874

Dianne Firth
craftact.org.au
0586, 0694, 0695, 0962

Dianne Gibson
0238–0241, 0351, 0409, 0462, 0463

Dominie Nash
dominienash.com
0474, 0863, 0864

Donna Blum
donna-seamstome.blogspot.com/
0563, 0659

Dorothy Heidemann-Nelson
0644

Eileen Doughty
DoughtyDesigns.com
0533

Eileen Williams
home.roadrunner.com/~eileenquilts
0539, 0540, 0615, 0619

Elaine Millar
elainemillarfiberworks.blogspot.com
0320, 0677

Elayne Novotny
0127

Eleanor A. McCain
0234-0237, 0346

Elena Stokes
elenastokes.com
0361

Elisabeth Nacenta-de la Croix
elisabethdelacroix.com
0436-0440

Elizabeth Barton
elizabethbarton.com
0585, 0931, 0951, 0966, 0968

Elizabeth F. Harris
0367, 0399-0401, 0967

Ellen Lindner
AdventureQuilter.com
0624, 0663, 0673, 0743, 0829, 0832

Ellen November
ellennovember.com
0820

Ellen Parrott
ellen-parrott.com
0635

Els Mommers
kunamola.blogspot.com
0621

Elsbeth Nusser-Lampe
elsbethnusserlampe.meinatelier.de
0471-0473

Emiko Toda Loeb
emikotloeb.com
0044-0046, 0097-0101

Enid Viljoen
enidviljoenquilts.jimdo.com
0903, 0904

Frances M. Snay
quiltsbyfransnay.com
0009, 0031

Franki Kohlaer
FrankiKohler.com
0603, 0428-0430, 0602

Frieda Oxenham
friedaquilter.blogspot.com
0258, 0297, 0379, 0381

Gail P. Sims
0122, 0798, 0799, 0884, 0926

Gay Young
gayyoungart.com
0468

Georgina Newson
rosecolouredworld.wordpress.com
0394, 0711

Geraldine A. Wilkins
livinh20.tumblr.com
0114, 0118, 0136, 0355

Geri deGruy
geridegruy.com
0211-0214, 0256, 0275, 0285-0289,
0317, 0358, 0360, 0362, 0363, 0366

Gerri Spilk
gerrispilka.com
0369-0372

Gillian Moss
mossartquilts.com
0662

Gillian Travis
gilliantravis.co.uk
0494, 0514, 0614

Gubser Adelheid
gubsera.ch
0390

Gunnel Hag
colourvie.com
0937

Gwen Goepel
0561

Gwendolyn Aqui-Brooks
blackartinamerica/fineart
0911

Heather DeBreuil
heatherdubreuil.com
0507, 0508

Heather Pregger
heatherquiltz.com
0700, 0701, 0704, 0705

Heidi Zielinski
heidizielinski.com
0330, 0916, 0925

Helen Remick
helenremick.com
0041-0043, 0321

Helene Kusnitz
helenekusnitz.com
0125, 0389, 0424, 0775

Henrietta L. Mac
0259, 0260

Hilde Morin
hildemorin.com
0250-0253, 0612

Holly Altman
hollyaltman.com
0478, 0885, 0886, 0930

Holly Brackmann
hollybrackmann.com
0221, 0222, 0404, 0451

Holly Knott
hollyknott.com
0643

Hope Wilmarth
hopewilmarth.com
0374, 0375, 0410, 0938

Hui-Fen Jessica Lin
jessicafabricfun.blogspot.tw
0674, 0944

Jamie Fingal
0454, 0729

Jana Lalova
lalova.cz/patchwork
0345, 0955, 0969

Jana Sterbova
janasterbova.com
0830, 0833, 0834

Janice Paine-Dawes
janicepainedawes.com
0845

Janie Krig
crazyvictoriana.etsy.com
0304

Janneke Van Der Ree
janneke.co
0610

Jean Brueggenjohann
0354

Jean Renli Jurgenson
fiberonthewall.com
0254, 0255

Jean Wells Keenan
jeanwellsquilts.com
0595, 0891, 0927

Jeanelle McCall
fivespoongallery.net
0609, 0641, 0651, 0876

Jeannie Palmer Moore
JPMArtist.com
0728

Jen Sorenson
aquiltedjewel.blogspot.com
0135

Jennifer Bowker
jennybowker.com
0652, 0653

Jennifer Hammond Landau
ruedoak.com
0594, 0760, 0889, 0890

Jenny K. Lyon
quiltskipper.com
0015, 0133, 0475, 0515

Jeri C. Pollock
0880, 0881, 0913

Jill Sheehan
0328

Jin-Gook Yang
0709

Joan Dyer
artful-women.blogspot.com
0242–0245, 0742

Joanne Alberda
wjalbrda.wix.com/joannealberdatextile
0422, 0870

Jodi Scaltreto
0054

Jolene Mershon
0107–0110, 0123, 0124, 0488

José Beenders
0050, 0051

Joy Nebo Lavrencik
joylavrencik.com
0846

Judith Content
judithcontent.com
0943

Judith Mundwiler
judithmundwiler.ch
0364, 0817, 0865, 0866

Judith Roderick
judithroderick.com
0516

Judy Cobillas
0933

Judy Doolan Kjellin
0134, 0888

Judy Paschalis
QuiltToonist.wordpress.com
0727

Julie Duschack
0486, 0487, 0749, 0804

Julie Haddrick
haddrickonfabric.com.au
0618

Julie R. Filatoff
jirafstudio.com
0702, 0797, 0908

Julie Snow
0849

K. Velis Turan
kvelisturan.com
0691–0693

Karen Farmer
karenfarmertextileart.com
0274, 0313, 0396, 0703

Karen Illman Miller
nautilus-fiberarts.com
0819

Karen Markley
0761

Karin Wallgren
0267, 0268

Katharina Litchman
ArtQuiltsByMietzi.com
0625, 0776

Katharine McColeman
0392

Kathi Everett
pearlstreetroad.blogspot.com
0596

Kathie Briggs
kathiebriggs.com
0481, 0636, 0716–0718

Kathleen Carrizal-Frye
0063–0069

Katie Pasquini Masopust
katiepm.com
0477, 0825, 0826, 0838

Kim Ritter
0446-0448

Kimberly Lapacek
PersimonDreams.com
0293, 0803

Klaske Witteveen
kittyquilt.blogspot.com
0033, 0034

Kristin La Flamme
kristinlaflamme.com
0052, 0339, 0395

Kristin Shields
kristinshields.typepad.com
0628

Laura Bisagna
lolobee.com
0115, 0352

Laurie Swim
laurieswim.com
0505, 0549

LaVerne Kemp
thewarpedweaver.blogspot.com
0593, 0899

Leni Levenson Wiener
leniwiener.com
0493, 0496-0498

LeRita McKeever
0025, 0057, 0077, 0078

Lin Hsin-Chen
linhsinchen.idv.tw/index.html
0655, 0707

Linda Anderson
laartquilts.com
0319

Linda Bilsborrow
lindabilsborrow.co.uk
0302, 0403

Linda Kittmer
lindakittmer.blogspot.ca
0055, 0310, 0522, 0733, 0734,
0736, 0737, 0827, 0828, 0912

Linda MacDonald
lindamacdonald.com
0499, 0500

Linda Robertus
lindarobertus.com
0315, 0316, 0329, 0495, 0502

Linda Stemer
BlueprintsOnFabric.com
0588

Lisa Corson
homespunheritage.com
0782, 0906, 0907

Lisa Walton
dyedheaven.com
0348

Lucy Carroll
lucycarrolltextiles.com
0491

Luisa Marina
0126, 0132

Lyric Montgomery Kinard
lyrickinard.com
0416, 0738, 0783-0785

Margaret (Meg) Filiatrault
0527, 0578, 0650, 0868

Margie Davidson
margiedavidson.ca
0382

Marianne Burr
marianneburr.com
0792-0796

Marianne R. Williamson
0517, 0542, 0634, 0732

Marijke van Welzen
art2wearblog.blogspot.com
0476, 0571, 0787

Marjolijn van Wijk
marjolijnquilts.blogspot.com
0029, 0030, 0070, 0547, 0666

Marjorie Post
thedragonflystudio.com
0323, 0324, 0415, 0678, 0877, 0878

Martha Ressler
martharessler.com
0506

Martha Wolfe
marthawolfe.com
0528-0531

Marti Plager
martiplager.com
0277-0279

Marven Donati
0082, 0419

Mary Ann Van Soest
cedarridgestudio.blogspot.com
0604-0606

Mary MacIlvain
maryart.macilvain.com
0414

Mary Markworth
0047, 0076, 0617, 0814, 0924, 0954

Mary Pal
MaryPalDesigns.com
0532

Mary T. Buchanan
0800-0802

Mary Tabar
marytabar.com
0005-0008, 552

Masae Harata
0119, 0120

Maxine Oliver
maxineoliver.blogspot.com
0562

Maya Schonenberger
mayaschonenberger.com
0600, 0601, 0671

Meg Cowey
0862

Melani Kane Brewer
melanibrewer.com
0483, 0544-0546

Melanie Grant
melaniegrantdesign.com
0010-0012, 0014, 0019, 0020, 0023,
0048, 0049, 0318, 0417, 0668

Melinda Sword
facebook.com/quiltedbymelinda
0649

Michele Sanandajian
urbanpalmstudios.com
0565, 0740, 0835–0837

Michelle Wilkie
factotum-of-arts.com
0290, 0291

Miriam Basart
miriambasart.com
0875

Miriam K. Sokoloff
0675

Nancy Bardach
nancybardach.com
0867

Nancy Billings
nancybdesigns.com
0841, 0843, 0956–0959

Nancy Dobson
nancydobson.com
0518, 0519, 0574, 0598, 0623,
0762, 0896

Nancy King
0640

Naomi S. Adams
killerbeedesigns.com
0909

Naomi Weidner
home.earthlink.net/~howl-moon
0646

Natalie Isvarin-Love
facebook.com/Natalies.Whim
0910

Nelda Warkentin
neldawarkentin.com
0778, 0779, 0963

Neroli Henderson
eiloren.blogspot.com.au
0597

Nienke Smit
nienkesmit.nl
0022, 0062, 0080, 0081, 0117

Noriko Endo
norikoendo.com
0432, 0433

Noriko Misawa
0102, 0103

Odette Tolksdorf
odettetolksdorf.co.za
0303, 0305, 0336, 0340, 0341, 0347,
0405, 0420, 0421, 0577, 0879

Pam Gantz
0061

Pamela Mansfield
0121, 0648

Pat Bishop
patbishop.info
0376, 0377, 0950

Pat Hertzberg
PatHertzberg.com
0567, 0844

Pat Kroth
krothfiberart.com
0807–0809, 0813

Pat Owoc
patowoc.com
0425

Patricia Charity
fromedge2edge.com
0388

Patricia Forster
0941

Patricia Gould
angelfiredesigns.com
0589, 0766

Patricia Kennedy-Zafred
pattykz.com
0501, 0503, 0504

Patricia Malarcher
0856, 0857, 0900

Patricia Scott
0672, 0898

Patt Blair
pattsart.com
0513

Penny Naquin Dant
0525, 0526

Phyllis Small
phyllissmall.com
0273, 0555, 0620

Randy Frost
0821, 0853, 0882, 0893–0895

Rebekah Dundon
bekahdu.com.au
0452, 0453

Rhoda Taylor
0378, 0380, 0406

Rhonda Baldwin
rhojobaldwin.wordpress.com
0520, 0731

Robbie Payne
robbiespawprints.blogspot.com
0088, 0322, 0901

Robin DeMuth Schofield
0356, 0357, 0730

Robin Ryan
0333

Robyn McGrath
0632

Rose Rushbrooke
roserushbrooke.com
0739

Roseline Young
roselineweaving.webs.com
0949

Roslyn DeBoer
0535, 0536

Ruth Christos
0215–0218

Sandy Campbell
0083

Sara Sharp
sarasharp.com
0484

Sarah Ann Smith
SarahAnnSmith.com
0141, 0541

Sarah Cullins
0027, 0028, 0058, 0060

Sarah Lykins Entsminger
0616

Shannon M. Conley
imworkingonaproject.blogspot.com
0426

Sharon Buck
sharonbuckart.weebly.com
0897

Sharon Casey
scaseyquilts.blogspot.com
0918, 0919

Sharon G. Cheney
0647

Sharon Wiley Hightower
0887

Sharon Willas Rubuliak
0261, 0262

Shea Wilkinson
sheawilkinson.com
0553, 0554, 0960, 0961

Sheila Frampton-Cooper
Zoombaby.com
0822-0824

Shelley Brucar
handmade-memories.com
0457, 0543, 0791

Shelly Burge
shellyburge.com
0094, 0111, 0112, 0226, 0257, 0292,
0296, 0298, 0301, 0334, 0343,
0344, 0391, 0764

Sheri Schumacher
behance.net/sherischumacher
0229-0233, 0411-0413

Sherri Lipman McCauley
SherriLipmanMcCauley.blogspot.com
0294, 0383

Shirley MacGregor
shirleymacgregor.com
0327

Shirley Mooney
dontwaittocreate.blogspot.nz
0534, 0939

Sion Thomas
0928

Sue Benner
suebenner.com
0712-0715

Sue Hotchkis
suehotchkis.com
0754-0756, 0932

Sue Reno
suereno.com
0469

Susan Fuller
fullerbydesign. com
0208-0210

Susan Jackan
0295

Susan L. Price
0661

Susan Selby
0575, 0629

Susan Shie
turtlemoon.com
0441-0444

Susan Wittrup
susanwittrup.com
0915

Suzanne Mouton Riggio
0590

Suze Termaat
suzetermaat.nl
0537

Sylvia Naylor
sylvianaylor.com
0458-0461

Sylvia Naylor
sylvianaylor.com
0630, 0631

Tafi Brown
tafibrown.com
0720-0726

Tanya A. Brown
tanyabrown.org
0427, 0480, 0638

Teresa Shippy
teresashippy.com
0580-0582

Terry Aske
terryaskeartquilts.com/Studio
0445, 0509-0512, 0658, 0664

Terry Waldron
terrywaldron.com
0325, 0326

Thelma Newbury
0521, 0572, 0573

Therese May
theresemay.com
0681-0684

Tierney Davis Hogan
tierneycreates.wordpress.com
0001-0004, 0247-0249

Toni Bergeon
0387, 0627, 0645

Uta Lenk
justquilts.de
0308

Valya
VALYAart.com
0735, 0831, 0920-0922

Vase of Tulips, c. 1930
0169

Veronica Oborn Jefferis
0228, 0431, 0633

Vicki Bohnhoff
0032, 0398

Vicki Conley
0131, 0353

Victoria Adams Brown
ribbonsmyth.com
0084-0087

Victoria Rondeau
ISewDesireQuilts.com
0639

Viktorya Allen
viktorya-art.blogspot.mx
0656

Vinda G. Robison
0564

Virginia A. Spiegel
VirginiaSpiegel.com
0744, 0788

Vita Marie Lovett
0654, 0815, 0816, 0818

Vivian Helena Aumond-Capone
vivianhelena.com
0225, 0365, 0467, 0748, 0902

W. Jean Ayres
0013, 0017, 0018, 0024, 0089,
0090–0093, 0095, 0096

Watanabe Kayoko
0104–0106

Wen Redmond
wenredmond.com
0685–0687, 0689, 0859–0861

Wendy Harris Williams
wendyharriswilliams.wix.com/
wendyharriswilliams
0331

Wendy Read
wendyread.com
0660, 0871

Wil Duyst
willijn.blogspot.nl
0035, 0036, 0039, 0040, 0113, 00128

Wil Opio Oguta
wilopiooguta.com
0665, 0842

Acknowledgments

I owe a debt of gratitude to all the participants in my quilt critique workshops during the past ten years, who increased my appreciation of quilts as an expressive medium, and to my teachers at the Institute of Fine Arts, New York University, who honed my critical abilities. To Martha Sielman, executive director of Studio Art Quilt Associates, I am grateful for her books showcasing contemporary quilt art, and to Karey Bresenhan and Nancy O'Bryant Puentes for their forty years of championing traditional quilts as an art form. This book would not have happened without the encouragement and professionalism of the Quarry team, especially Jonathan Simcosky and Betsy Gammons. Finally, I thank my husband for his patience during our many dinners while I "talk quilts."

For my own studio quilts created during the past thirty-five years, I wish to acknowledge the inspiration of works by Anna Atkins, Tafi Brown, Hannah Höch, Wendy Huhn, Christopher James, Yvonne Porcella, Robert Rauschenberg, Lucas Samaras, and Rosie Lee Tomkins. Also, I learned photo transfer from the books of Jean Ray Laury, and photographer Diane Neumaier taught me how to print cyanotype on fabric in 1979.